About Your Instructors

Patrice Bonnell

Patrice Bonnell is a forward thinking, results-driven coach who has gained 20 years of success assisting hundreds of small and large practices achieve immediate growth, create effective management protocols, strengthen leadership abilities, dramatically improve communication skills, increase income and create more time to do the things dentists and team members truly desire to do.

Shelly Goff

Shelly Goff is a dedicated and vibrant coach with over 20 years in the dental industry. She has worked closely with hundreds of dentists and specializes in customized marketing and team building.

Table of Contents

Who We Are

Rate Your Practice

This short inventory will reveal how your practice measures up in terms of service. Read each statement, and circle the number that represents how strongly you agree or disagree with each statement. 5 represents "Strongly Agree" and 1 represents "Strongly Disagree."

Item	1 = Disagree 5 = Agree				
New Patient Interaction					
All staff knows the practice website address.	1	2	3	4	5
All staff knows the menu of services your practice offers.	1	2	3	4	5
A live person answers the telephone within three rings.	1	2	3	4	5
The person answering the telephone is pleasant and efficient.	1	2	3	4	5
You seldom – if ever -- use the answering machine during office hours.	1	2	3	4	5
You follow a precise protocol and script to gather information whenever a new patient calls.	1	2	3	4	5
You schedule new patients within one week of their initial call, if possible.	1	2	3	4	5
You send a welcome letter or email personally signed by the doctor to new patients prior to the appointment (if time allows), or within 3 days after.	1	2	3	4	5
You schedule new patients to arrive early so there is plenty of time to fill out required forms.	1	2	3	4	5
The doctor personally calls new patients the day before the appointment to welcome them to the practice.	1	2	3	4	5
The practice allows patients to include a cleaning on their first visit.	1	2	3	4	5
Each Morning Huddle includes an announcement of new patient names and appointment times.	1	2	3	4	5
The doctor learns the patient's chief complaints and goals before the exam.	1	2	3	4	5

Item	1 = Disagree 5 = Agree				
The doctor meets each new patient somewhere other than the treatment room.	1	2	3	4	5
All staff makes a point to warmly greet and welcome new patients (even if they're not scheduled to treat them).	1	2	3	4	5
All treatment partners follow specific protocols for the handoff, and personally escort the patient to each station.	1	2	3	4	5
As patients exit the office, every staff member in the area says "good-bye."	1	2	3	4	5
You send each new patient a thank-you note or email, personally signed by the doctor, immediately after the first visit.	1	2	3	4	5
(Total possible score for New Patient Interaction: 90) – YOUR SUBTOTAL:					

Office Appearance					
Exterior lights are off during daylight hours.	1	2	3	4	5
Office signage is clean, consistent, and professional.	1	2	3	4	5
The parking lot is well marked and free of litter.	1	2	3	4	5
The building exterior is fresh, clean, and well maintained.	1	2	3	4	5
Walls are clean with updated art, posters, or pictures.	1	2	3	4	5
Floors are clean (free of scuffmarks and stains) and updated.	1	2	3	4	5
The windows are clean.	1	2	3	4	5
The doors are free of scuffmarks and dirty handprints [if the door is glass, it is free of fingerprints].	1	2	3	4	5
All lights are on and working in the office.	1	2	3	4	5
The light fixtures are clean and free of dust, insects, or other debris.	1	2	3	4	5
(Total possible score for Office Appearance: 50) – YOUR SUBTOTAL:					

Patient Amenities

You reserve prominent, clearly marked parking spaces for your patients.	1	2	3	4	5
You do not make patients "sign in" when they arrive.	1	2	3	4	5
Your reception area is clean, tidy, and has up-to-date décor.	1	2	3	4	5
The magazines in your reception area are well-displayed, current and replaced when worn.	1	2	3	4	5
Your reception area includes educational materials (brochures, booklets, treatment descriptions) for your patients.	1	2	3	4	5
You offer patients complimentary umbrellas if it is raining, or escort them to their transportation if it is snowing or icy.	1	2	3	4	5
You offer waiting patients bottled water, coffee or tea, or other refreshment.	1	2	3	4	5
Your office restrooms are clean, well-stocked, and checked often for amenities.	1	2	3	4	5
You provide complimentary toothbrushes, toothpaste, and mouthwash in the restrooms.	1	2	3	4	5
You provide blankets in cool treatment rooms.	1	2	3	4	5
You provide warm moist facecloths during treatment.	1	2	3	4	5
You provide earphones, video, or other distracting entertainment for the patient in the treatment chair.	1	2	3	4	5
(Total Score possible for Patient Amenities: 60) – YOUR SUBTOTAL:					
Patient Interaction					
Your staff turns off their cell phones during office hours.	1	2	3	4	5
You and your staff do not conduct personal conversations in the presence of your patients.	1	2	3	4	5
Your hygienist or dental assistant converses with patients most often about dentistry in particular, avoiding mindless small talk.	1	2	3	4	5
Once you and your patient agree on a treatment plan, you or your staff escort the patient to a private setting to discuss financial arrangements.	1	2	3	4	5

You speak to your patients in terms of monthly payments, rather than discussing large dollar amounts.	1	2	3	4	5
You and your staff describe dental procedures in everyday language to make sure patients understand their treatment.	1	2	3	4	5
You provide patients with a copy of their treatment plan and financial arrangements at the time of acceptance.	1	2	3	4	5
You and the patient agree to financial arrangements in advance, before the next appointment is set.	1	2	3	4	5
You rarely, if ever, leave patients alone in the treatment room.	1	2	3	4	5
Your office stays on schedule and patients seldom wait more than 5 - 7 minutes in the reception area.	1	2	3	4	5
(Total Score possible for Patient Interaction: 50) – YOUR SUBTOTAL:					
Add all your subtotals to get your final score:					

Rating Your Service:

First, look at the total possible score for each section. If your subtotals are less than the total possible score, you can easily see areas for improvement. Next, add all your subtotals to get a total score.

If Your Total Score is:

225-250 Congratulations! You are providing excellent, 5-Star Service!

176-224 You are practicing Good, 4-Star Patient Service. Look at those areas you rated less than 5, and make just a few improvements to reach 5-Star Service.

126-175 You are providing basic, 3-Star Patient Service. Develop and implement a plan to improve those areas you rated 3 or less.

125 or less At best, you are providing 2-Star Patient Service. Immediately prioritize a complete overhaul of your customer service program.

Which employee are you?
AVERAGE EMPLOYEES
Come to work just for the paycheck
No desire to learn new things
Don't read
Resist change
Don't plan
Blame or justify
Motivated out of fear
Poor health habits
Never contribute new ideas
Love wasting time
TEAM
Poor teammates
A drag to be around
GREAT EMPLOYEES
Love doing great work
Constant learners
Read regularly
Embrace change
Plan for success
Motivated by a sense of excellence
Takes responsibility
Great health habits
Idea machine
Hate wasting time
Team leader
Fun to be around

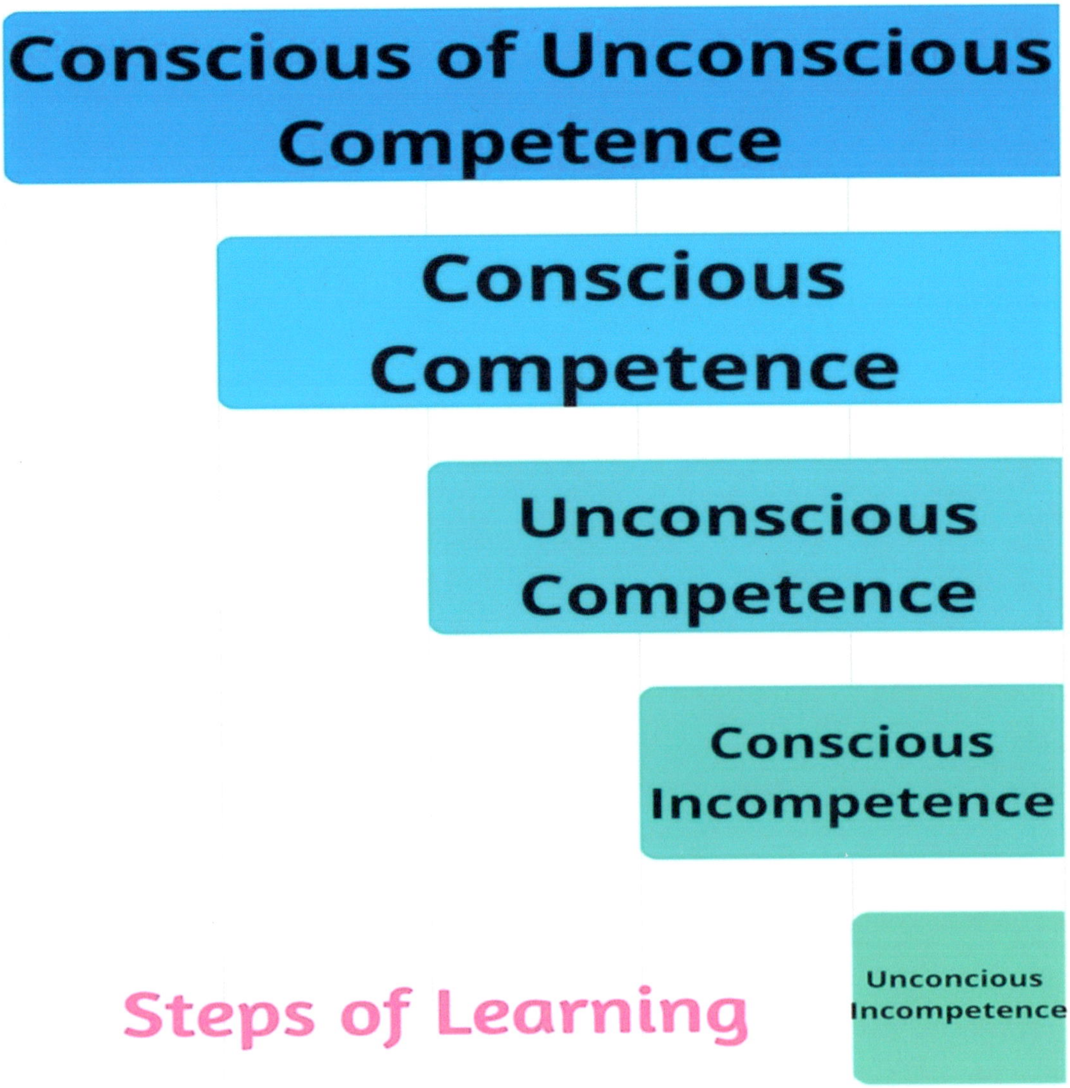
Conscious of Unconscious Competence
Conscious Competence
Unconscious Competence
Conscious Incompetence
Unconcious Incompetence
Steps of Learning

The 4 Stages of Learning

1. Unconscious Incompetence – That simply means that you don't know that you don't know! When you are not aware that you do not know something.

The best example of this is a young child.

2. Conscious Incompetence – That is when you begin to be aware that you do not know something. You start to recognize your lack of experience or your lack of knowledge in a particular area or endeavor of life. You recognize the fact that other people seem to know how to do things that you do not seem know how to do.

A good example of this would be teenagers who want to get a driver's license. They see other people driving a car and they want to drive one too!

3. Conscious Competence – This is the area where a person realizes that not only can they learn information, but they can also do something with it. They begin to practice and develop their skills. They get good at what they have learned how to do.

An example of this may be someone who can play the piano. They know what it takes to play the piano because they have practiced over and over again. And, the more they practiced, the more competent they become in that skill.

Anyone who is an expert at whatever they are doing has developed conscious competence. They put in the time, effort and energy to learn what it was they wanted to do in order to become more accomplished at doing it.

4. Unconscious Competence – This is when something becomes second nature to us. You no longer have to think about what you are doing. You can do it "in your sleep".

For instance, this could be as simple as riding a bicycle or driving a car or as complex as flying a plane. But, since you have done it for so many years you just get in and take off. You do not even give it a second thought.

This is the stage where a person makes whatever they are doing look very, very easy to everyone else. I think of a skilled chef who, after years of cooking, can make preparing a delicious meal look very easy. It truly is second nature to them because it has become a natural part of their life.

Truly this is the goal that we should all strive for – to get a place that whatever we do in life it just becomes second nature to us.

Please remember that all four of these stages of learning take time. Why not check to see where you think you might be in a particular area at this current time? If you need to grow, feel free to do so! If you want to begin a new area of life, don't feel badly that you have to start at the bottom of the ladder. It is in taking that first step that you begin to move up the ladder and get to where you want to go.

Plan for Success – aka: Empowerment

C > E

(Cause) (Effect)*

Results vs Reasons

Cause LEADS to Effect

Be AT Cause or be at the Mercy of Effects

What results DO you want?

Seek to see "How CAN I" as as opposed to "Why I can't"

Empowerment is: Moving from Effect to Cause and operating from a physiology to a psychology of *excellence*.

*If there is an area of life that isn't working for you, you are likely being at effect of something or someone

YOU CAN HAVE

RESULTS

- OR -

EXCUSES

NOT BOTH

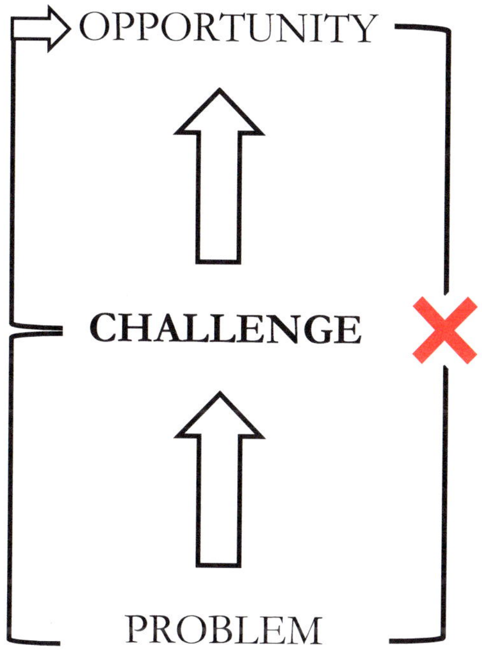
OPPORTUNITY
CHALLENGE
PROBLEM

Utilizing Your Multiple Personalities

For each personality, think of someone you know and list the positive traits associated with that personality.

Personality #1 The People Pleaser

____

Name

Positive Attributes

____

____

____

Personality #2 The Thinker

____

Name

Positive Attributes

____

____

____

Personality #3 The Achiever

____

Name

Positive Attributes

____

____

____

Personality #4 The Initiator

____

Name

Positive Attributes

____

____

____

- ~ You are primarily one personality yet you can access and utilize all four.
- ~ We are all capable of being whom we need to be to get what we want. Learn to activate all of these personalities in every situation.

The Learning State

Imagine you can download information to your memory easily and effortlessly with improved recall.

Being able to:

- Focus and concentrate
- Remember pertinent facts
- Think in compelling and constructive ways
- Prepare for tests and exams
- Banish nerves on command

This is about quieting and stilling your mind and switch form an analytical (conscious) form to a more relaxed (subconscious) form.

The Learning State is a resourceful state for learning where you widen the use of your senses in order to increase your ability to take in more information from your surroundings, as well as, utilize and store information.

The Technique:

1. Pick a spot above your eye line in front of you. Focus on that spot, taking in all the colors, textures, lights, shadows, etc. Take a deep breath and relax into it.
2. Allow your vision to slowly expand out so that you are looking at the spot and seeing each side of the room, slowly take your vision out a little more until you can't focus on the spot, yet you can see your hands if you stretch your arms out level with your shoulders.
3. Now stretch your vision even wider. Stretch your awareness in your imagination to as far around you as you can. Now you're in peripheral vision.

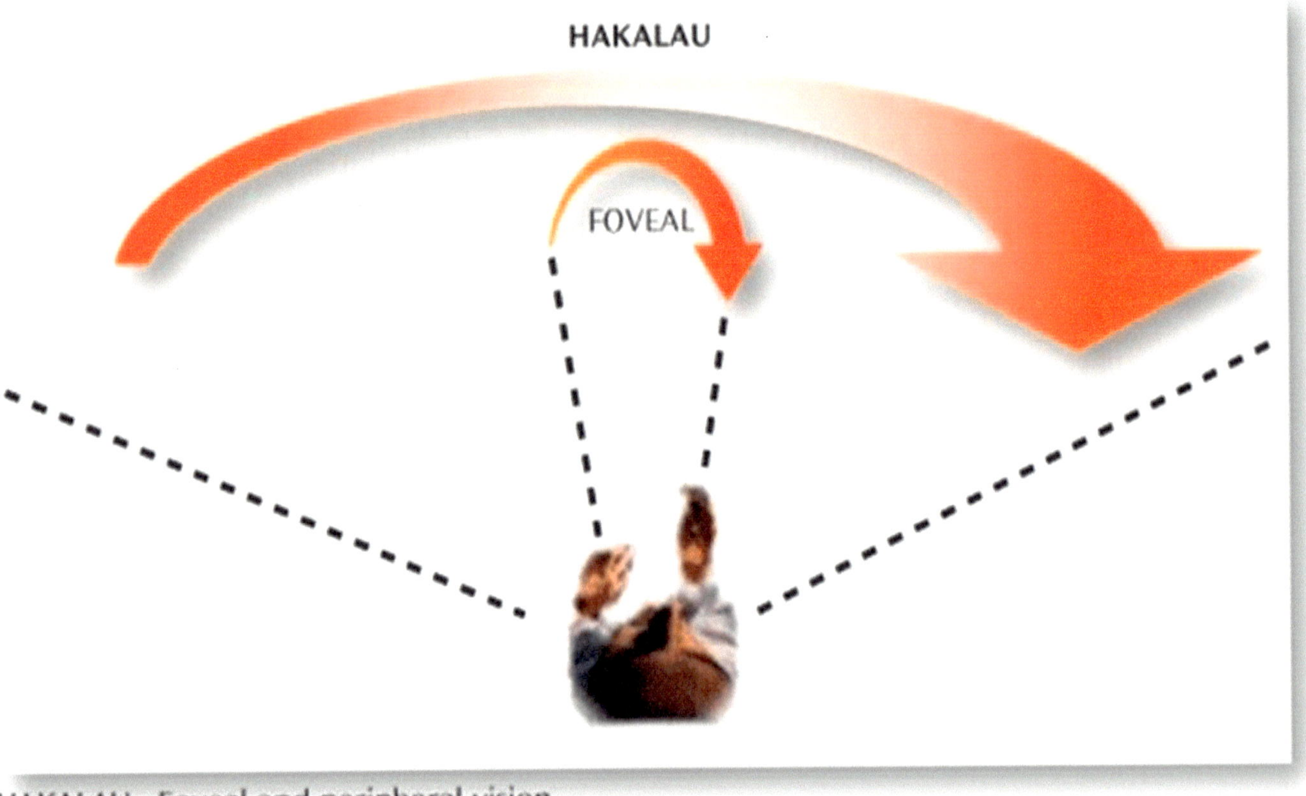

HAKALAU - Foveal and peripheral vision

Why Choose Us?

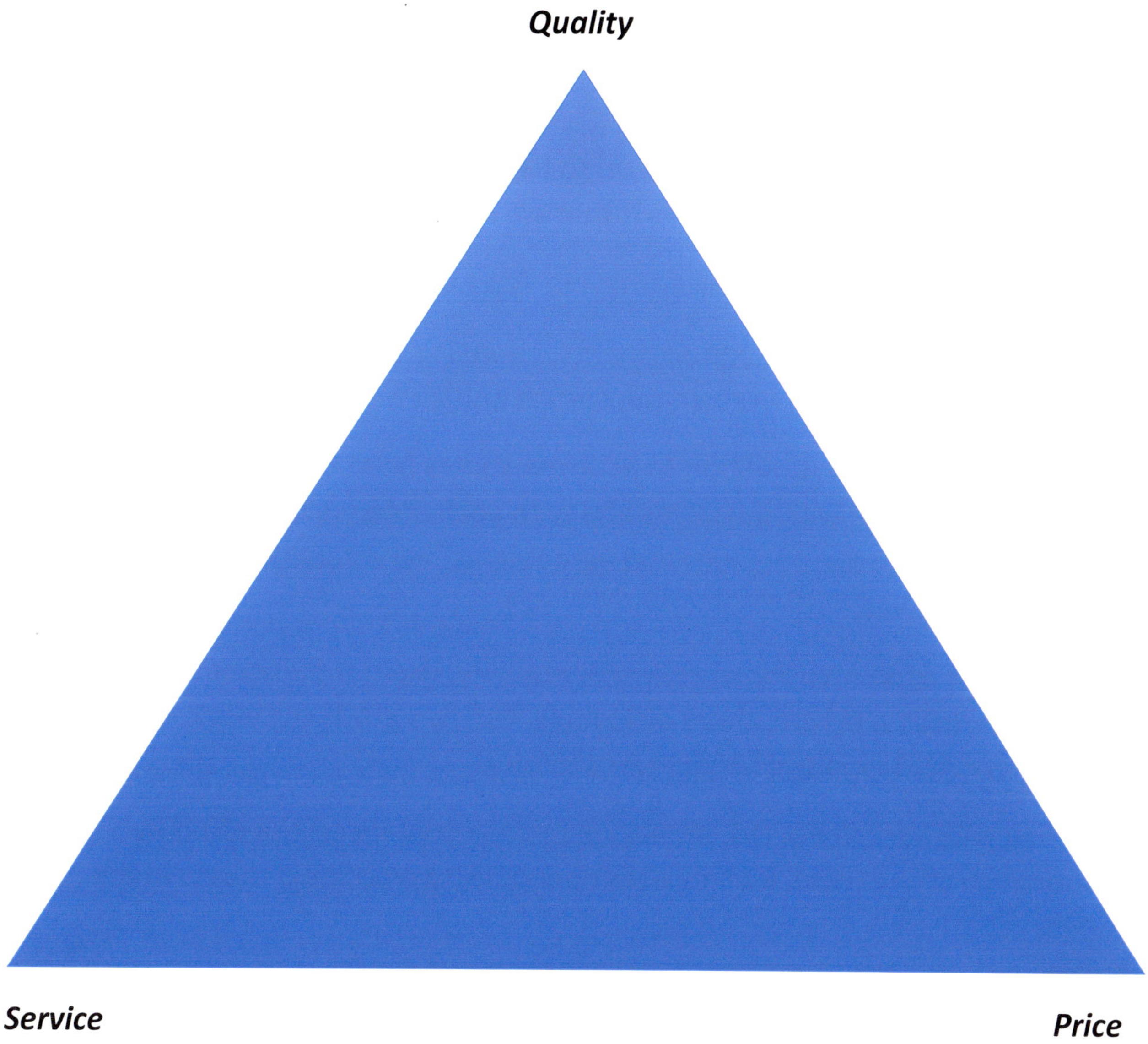

Managing Systems, NOT People

When was the last time you experienced frustration at the office? What event led to that frustration? Is it frustrating when others do not follow through with what they say they are going to do?

We can chalk these disappointments up to two things: Missing Agreements or Broken Agreements. The good news is that we can manage both.

Managing by Systems = Managing via Agreements:

Many of our frustrations, disappointments, as well as chaos between team members, originates from miscommunication and/or misunderstandings.

Success in our business is built on trust. Trust comes from the decisions and agreements we make with ourselves and with each other. When we choose to follow through with our decisions and agreements, we establish integrity for our teams and ourselves.

Upholding our agreements ensures accountability, desired outcomes and measurable results. In turn, these outcomes lead to a gratifying work environment AND employee/employer security.

Managing with agreements vs. managing people, centers on the effective performance of the team. It eliminates unnecessary emotional upsets in the workplace.

How it works

Most agreements in our practices are expected or unnoticed—UNTIL they are broken and frustration arises.

Agreement always include:

1. WHAT the expectation or desired result is
2. WHO the commitment involves or could involve
3. WHERE the agreement is to be executed
4. HOW the commitment should be carried out, if there are pertinent specifications
5. WHEN is the commitment completion date (By-When)

Agreements Tracker

This final component is really the key to the success of this system. The tracker should be customized to suit the needs of the team. It can be as simple as a designated notebook or a tracking document on the computer. Tracking these commitments keeps the entire team in INTEGRITY, on track, moving forward, resulting in peace, harmony and more effective use of the team's time and energy, creating a 5-Star Experience for your patients.

The agreement tracker is managed by one team member to maintain accountability, continuity and accountability.

The difference between managing with systems vs managing people is that the focus is placed on the condition of your commitments and performance and not personality or personal preferences. This system allows work to be work, removing the more personal, sometimes distracting emotional upsets from the work environment.

Mindset

Real Influence is about Leadership

The Middle

"Everything's Okay As Long As It's Okay,

And Everything Is Okay

Until Okay Isn't Okay Anymore."

Think of someone you admire or look up to. How does that person do things? How does that person make decisions? How does that person take action?

When you break it down to different pieces of the puzzle that makes up that person, you will get a clearer picture of how that person lives their life.

Most people live in the ***middle.***

What does that mean to you?

Most people live in their comfort zone, their Okay zone.

The challenge is those same people will defend where they're at even though it's not where they want to be. You will notice that LEADERS do Not live in the middle. They step away from the herd.

You can **Choose** to be the leader of your outcomes and be at **Cause** or you can stay stuck in the middle with the rest of the herd.

Which Do YOU choose?

The 3 Requisites for Change

1. Eliminate Negative Emotions and Limiting Decisions, Integrate Parts and Create a Compelling Future

In the Office

Out of the Office

2. Take Action--Includes Enforcing Your Boundaries
3. Focus on What You Want--Remember, Your Evaluations Become Suggestions To Your Unconscious Mind

What's the Difference?

Reality	Limiting Decision
-I don't have any money	-I can't make money
-I don't love anyone	-I can't love
-I don't trust anyone	-It's not okay to trust
-I'm not athletic	-I can't develop athletic ability
-I don't dance well	-I can't dance
-I suck at having relationships working for	-Relationships aren't worth
-People lie to me and that hurts	-I don't yet have enough sensory acuity to know when I'm being lied to
-Doing taxes is boring	-I can't discipline myself
-Exercise is hard	-Exercise isn't worth my time

The Comfort Zone

- Your comfort zone is your prison
- Within it is everything in your life
- Everything you want in your life that you don't yet have lies outside of your comfort zone
- To live a truly fulfilled life, you have to learn to step out of your comfort zone
- This means, embracing fear and turning it into enthusiasm
- So. That means, we're going to get out of our Comfort Zones this week!

The Importance of Your Focus

You need to be in charge of your focus and your results.

We at Transform Destiny are caring people, and you also need to know that we don't care about your excuses for not having, being, or doing what you want and having your life the way you want it.

We invite you to give up arguing for your limitations.

Taking Responsibility

In life, there are things that happen *to* you and things that happen *because* of you. One you have control of, the other you don't.

The things that happen *to* you is often out of your control:

Boss or team member in a bad mood
Car does not start
Economy is ruining my business

Many things in life we cannot control BUT can we influence them? Do you spend your time wasting energy worrying about it or do you create positive change?

The things that happen *because* of you and your actions are 100% in your control.

THE KEY IS PERSONAL RESPONSIBILITY

When you live in Effect, you live in constant excuses for poor results and unsatisfying outcomes. When you take *Responsibility* for what is happening around you and in your life, you put yourself in a position of **Power** (Cause) from which you can achieve your desired outcomes and goals. You are solie responsible for the VALUE you get out of life.

Cause is a position of empowerment. *Cause* is:

- Taking responsibility for creating what you want in your life and deciding what you achieve.
- Taking ownership in the belief that life is an ocean of opportunities rather than constant obstacles holding you back.
- Accepting you have a choice about who you are, what you do, how you show up for yourself and others and how you react to other people, their emotions and the responses you receive.
- Taking 100% responsibility in your communication with yourself and others.
- Taking 100% responsibility how others perceive your words.
- Taking 100% responsibility in your actions.

You have a choice. Which side do you choose

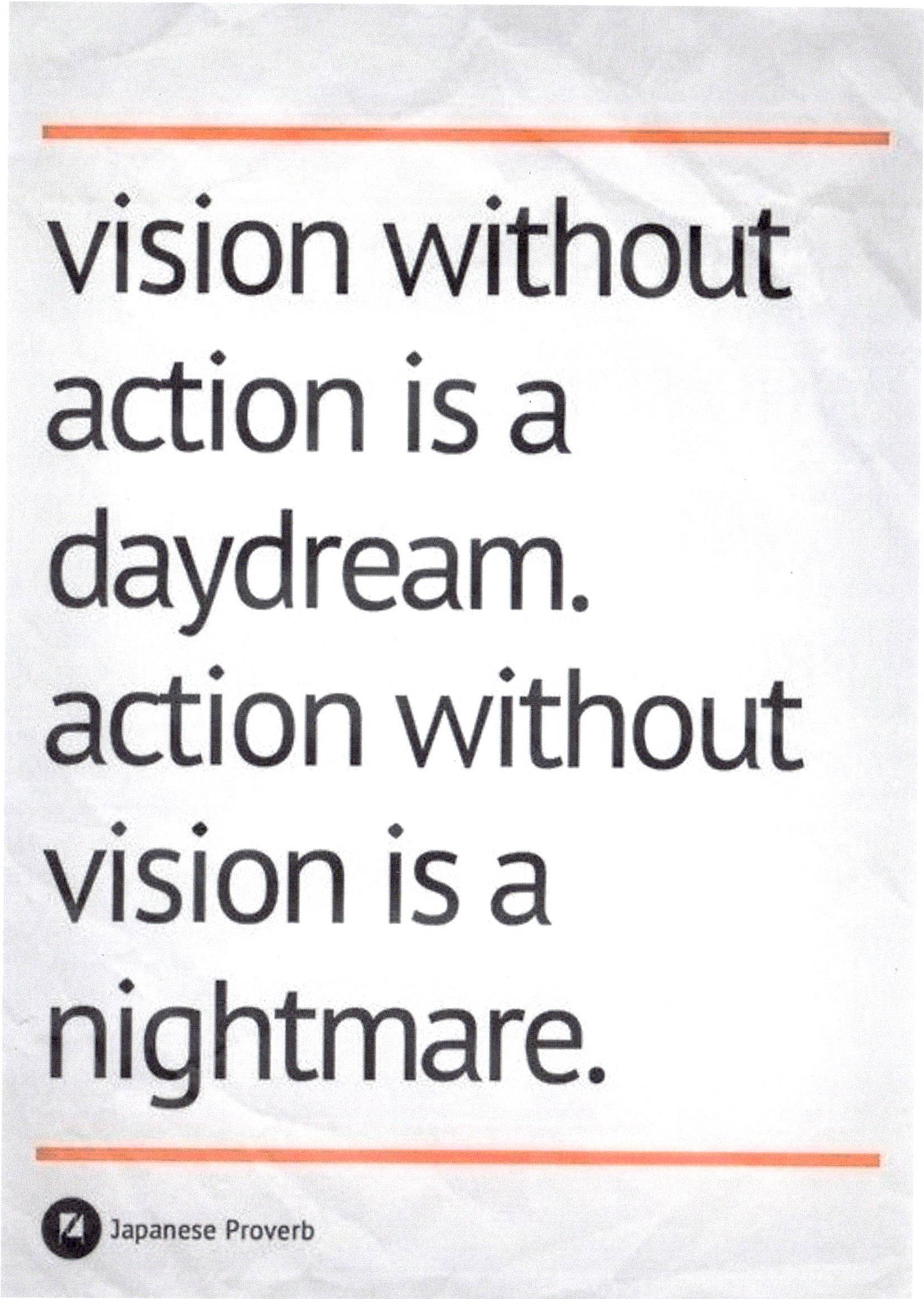
vision without action is a daydream.
action without vision is a nightmare.
Japanese Proverb

ACTIONS PROVE WHO SOMEONE IS, WORDS JUST PROVE WHO THEY WANT TO BE

Unknown...

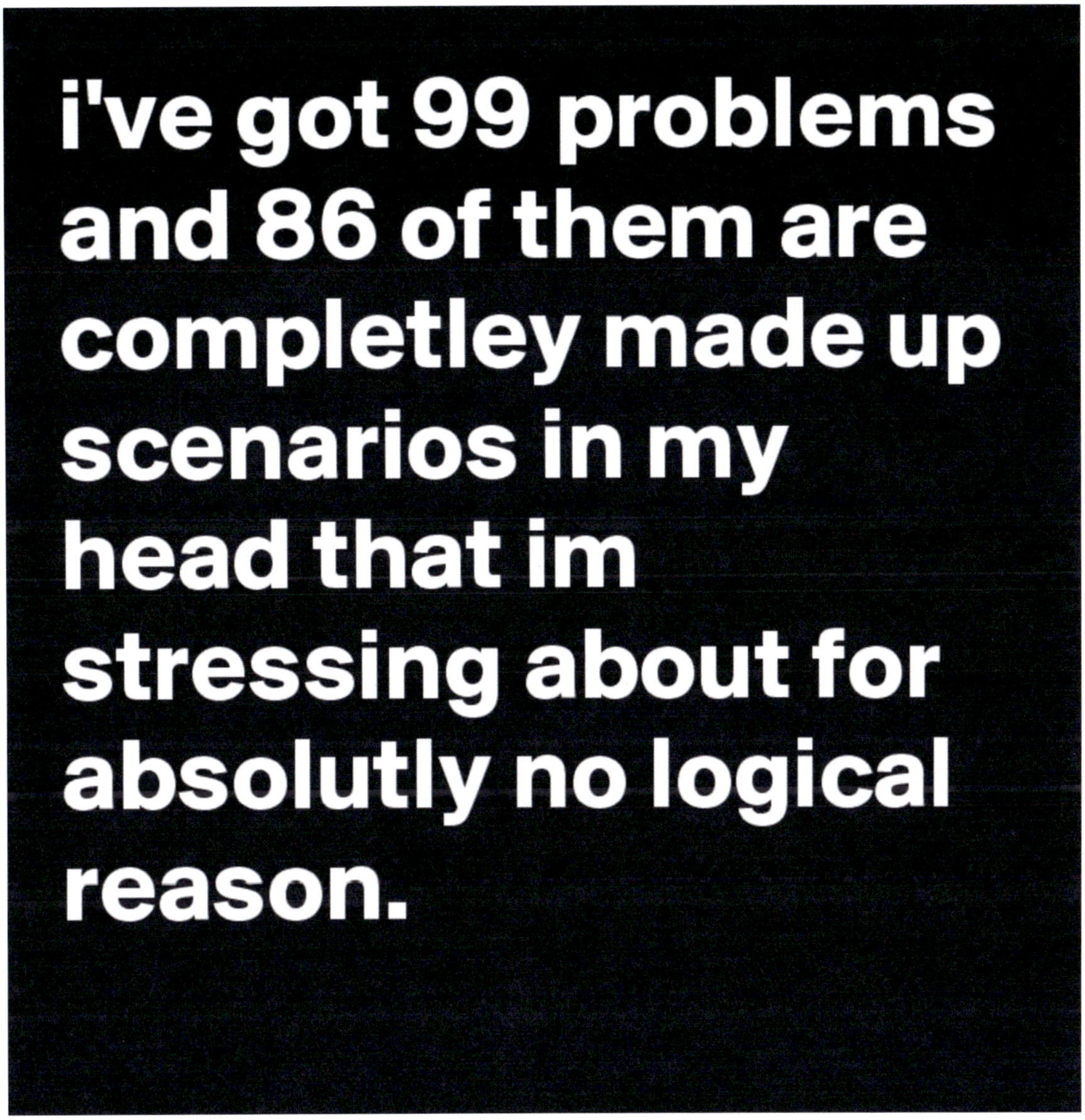
i've got 99 problems and 86 of them are completley made up scenarios in my head that im stressing about for absolutly no logical reason.

When you stop being

Right,

You stop making everyone

Else wrong

AND

We can all start LIVING!

16 Core Beliefs to Create Change & Empower Communication

1. Behavior is the best bit of information about a person.
2. People are Not their behavior/actions. People are just Doing their behavior. You are not the label you or others call you, you are doing the label's behavior.
3. Every behavior/action has a positive intention behind it.
4. Emotions are facts in the moment. (I feel angry vs. I am angry)
5. There are no difficult people, just difficult relationships and people being inflexible.
6. We all have our own internal map of reality; people respond to theirs Not yours.
7. People respond to their experiences, not to reality itself.
8. Having a choice is better than not having a choice. Always give people options if you want to shift them.
9. People make the best choices they can at any given time.
10. People work perfectly.
11. The unconscious mind balances the conscious mind (All change takes place in the unconscious mind).
12. The meaning of communication is not what you say, it's the response you get from others.
13. People have all the resources they need….. or they can create them.
14. We process all information through our senses.
15. If someone has already done something, we can model their action to achieve the same result.
16. If you want to understand, act.

Oral Systemic

Healthy Mouth Standard of Care

Patients, unfortunately, are not typically aware of how to create and maintain a healthy mouth. Nor, do they usually understand how important a healthy mouth is to their overall health.

A patient's mouth is a window into their overall health. By understanding the health of a patient's mouth, we can understand his or her overall health. For example, inflammation in a patient's mouth is a clear indicator of inflammation in his or her vital organs.

More importantly, problems within the mouth are now linked to a variety of problems in a patient's vital organs. For example, gum disease is linked to increases in:

- Heart disease
- Strokes
- Diabetes
- Preterm and low-weight births
- Respiratory problems
- Osteoporosis
- Rheumatoid arthritis
- Gastric Ulcers
- Pancreatic and prostate cancers, and even
- Alzheimer's

The Healthy Mouth Standard creates an advanced responsibility with our patient's total health and wellness

So let's create our Healthy Mouth Standard of Care.

A Healthy Mouth

Oral Pain
Oral Infections
Bad Breath/Taste
Bleeding
Crowded Teeth
Red and/or Swollen Gums
Missing Teeth
Gum Disease
A Healthy Mouth is freedom from...
Fractured Teeth
Cavities
Oral Cancer
Gum Recession
Dry Mouth
Jaw/Joint Problems
Frequent Headaches
Loose Teeth
Excessive Tooth Wear

A Healthy Mouth Is Freedom From:

- ~ Bleeding
- ~ Decay (cavities)
- ~ Inflammation
- ~ Pain
- ~ Infection
- ~ Bad Breath
- ~ Crowding
- ~ Missing Teeth
- ~ Fractures
- ~ Cancer

What Happens in Your Mouth...Does Not Stay in Your Mouth

The Oral-Systemic Facts

Your mouth talks to your body...

- At least 80% of American adults have gum inflammation/ disease.
- Gum disease is linked with blood vessel disease, heart attacks and strokes.
- Gum disease and tooth loss increases risk of Alzheimer's disease.
- If you have diabetes and bleeding gums, your risk of premature death increases by 400 to 700 percent.
- Gum disease increases risk for head & neck cancer, and pancreatic and kidney cancer.

...and your body talks to your mouth!

- Increased trigeminal nerve traffic from TMJ and bad dental bite can create central sensitization and migraines.
- Poor ventilation during sleep triggers nighttime clenching and bracing to maintain the airway.
- Bad bites and poor oral-facial development increases risk for sleep apnea.
- Cavities are caused by acid-loving bacteria spread during kissing and sharing food.
- Oral bacteria are being found in brain tissue, heart vessels, joints, and many other parts of your body.

Communication

Building Rapport

Rapport is the foundation for meaningful interaction between people. Everyone knows how important good communication and trust are when building relationships with your patients. When you have rapport with another person, you have the opportunity to enter their world and see things from their perspective, feel how they are feeling and understand where they are coming from.

It is about understanding, respecting and honoring a person's model of the world. When you establish this, it creates a space for your patients to feel listened to, heard and understood. In turn, they will be more open to your suggestions. Have you ever thought about what it takes to build instant rapport with anyone?

Rapport is one of the most influential components of every unconscious human communication. It is the ability to connect with others in a way that creates trust and understanding from the very first interaction, whether it be over the phone or face-to-face. It is the ability to see and understand another's point of view (state) and guide them to understand yours.

The majority of decisions we make each day are contingent on the rapport created with us (visually, kinesthetically, auditorily) and the emotions we attach to that experience.

Patient Modalities

Patients have different modalities. Some are Visual. Some are Kinesthetic. Others are Auditory or Auditory Digital. By understanding the different modalities, you can adapt your approach to each patient in order to help build rapport.

Visual (40% of Population)

- You should be organized, neat and well groomed. Patients with a visual modality want to look good. And they expect the same from you.
- These patients use visualization for memory and decision-making - often getting insights about something.
- They are more imaginative and may have difficulty putting their ideas in words.
- They speak faster than the general population. Why? Because they have a picture(s) in their mind and if it is a moving picture, there is a lot to tell in so little time!
- They prefer in-person interactions - to see the other person and his/her reactions.
- They may seem to talk about disjointed topics. Why? Because they see the whole picture and it is easy to jump around to different parts of it.
- They may have difficulty putting their ideas in words. Why? Because there is so much they see in their minds.
- They want to see or be shown concepts, ideas or how something is done. They want to see the big picture.
- They may not remember what people have said and become confused if you give them too many verbal instructions. However, if you can draw a map or picture for them, then they can see what you are saying.
- They remember faces more easily than names.
- They may be distracted by visual activity and less so by noise.
- They are attracted to pictures, x-rays, models, imaging, drawings, visual descriptions and visual words.

Kinesthetic (40% of Population)

- Kinesthetic patients tend to speak slower than the general population. Why? Because they need time to get in *touch* with how they *feel* about the topic.
- They may be more sensitive to their bodies and their *feelings* and respond to *physical* rewards and *touching*.
- They learn by *doing*, *moving* or *touching*.
- They dress and groom themselves more for *comfort* than how they look.
- They make decisions based on their *feelings*.
- They stand closer to other people than those with a visual preference - to *feel* the other person's *energy*, whereas the person with a visual preference will stand back to see more of the other person (body language, etc.).
- They take on other people's feelings and make them their own.
- They feel emotions such as love/hurt deeply.
- They are emotionally driven and responsive to soft touch, tenderness, temperature and pain. They have less interest in intra-oral pictures. However, they like to touch and feel models.

Auditory (10% of Population)

- Auditory Patients will be more aware of subtle changes in the *tone* of your voice and be more responsive to certain *tones* of voice.
- They perceive and represent sequences and are able to remember directions or instructions more easily.
- They learn by *listening* and *asking* questions.
- They enjoy *discussions* and prefer to communicate through *spoken* language rather than the written word.
- They *talk* through problems and like to have someone available to serve as a *sounding* board for their ideas.
- They need to be *heard*.
- They are easily distracted by *noise*.
- They love to talk, love verbal communication, want explanations for everything, are more social and are greatly affected by spoken words.
- They like to have others listen to them.
- Auditory patients have a tendency to lose interest when clinicians and treatment coordinators overuse visual tools and demonstrations.

Auditory Digital (10% of Population)

The auditory digital system is not related to any of our senses. Instead of saying something "looks good," "sounds right," "feels nice," or "tastes good", a person with a preference for auditory digital may say, "this makes sense," "is logical" or "the specifications are correct."

- Auditory Digital patients have a need to make *sense* of the world, to *figure* things out, to *understand*.
- They *talk to themselves* and carry on conversations with you in their mind. Often they will say they remember discussing something with you, when you actually did not have the conversation. They did, however, in their mind!
- They need to *speak eye to eye* to *get responses.*
- They learn by working things out in their mind.
- They tend not to be spontaneous, as they like to *think* things through.
- They allow *logic* to play a key role in the *decision* process. They also rely on *facts* and *figures*.
- They memorize by steps, procedures, and sequences.
- They may do or say the same thing over and over.
- Auditory digital patients understand when you explain treatment in order of Mandatory, Elective and Cosmetic. It makes sense as far as what should be treated first, second and third.

Visual	Auditory	Kinesthetic	AD/Labelling
Memorize by seeing pictures and are less distracted by noise. Often have trouble remembering and are bored by long verbal 'instructions' because their minds may wander. They are interested in how the program looks.	Typically, are easily distracted by noise. They can repeat things back to you easily and learn by listening. They like music and like to talk on the phone. Tone of voice and the words used can be important.	Often they talk slowly and breathy. They respond to physical rewards and touching. They memorize by doing or walking through something. They will be interested in a program that feels right or gives them a gut feeling.	They spend a fair amount of time talking to themselves. They memorize by steps, procedures, sequences. They will want to know the program makes sense. They can also sometimes exhibit characteristics of other modalities.
• See • Look • Clear • Picture • Imagine • Focused • View • Appear • Show • Dawn • Reveal • Envision • Illuminate • Foggy • Hazy • Crystal • Bright • An eyeful • Tunnel Vision	• Hear • Listen • Sound(s) • Tell • Make music • Harmonize • Tune in/out • Be all ears • Rings a bell • Clear as a bell • Silence • Be heard • Resonate • Deaf • Mellifluous • Dissonance • Hush • Unhearing • Roar	• Feel • Touch • Grasp • Get hold of • Slip through • Solid • Catch on • Tap into • Make contact • Throw out • Turn around • Hard • Unfeeling • Concrete • scrape • get a handle • solid • Pull some strings • Get a hold	• Sense • Experience • Understand • Think • Know • Learn • Process • Decide • Motivate • Consider • Change • Perceive • Insensitive • Distinct • Conceive • Know • Perceive • Question • Distinct

Representational System Metaphors

Visual Metaphors

I see what you mean.
I want a different perspective.
Try to see things my way.
I have a vision of how things could be.
Things are looking up.
Shed some light on the matter.
I am trying to picture it.
Clear as mud.
Let's look at this closely.
The outlook is dim.
Seeing eye to eye.
It's not yet clear.

Auditory Metaphors

We're on the same wavelength.
Speaking the same language.
Tune in to this.
I hear what you are saying.
I like your story.
Lost for words.
Living in harmony.
Talking gobbledygook.
Quiet as a mouse.
Sounds good.
Turn a deaf ear.
Strikes a chord.

Kinesthetic Metaphors

I'm ready to tackle this head on.
I've got a feel for the place.
He wants something concrete.
Maintaining a sense of balance.
He rubs me the wrong way.
A cool customer.
Things just flowed.
Get a grip on yourself.
Can you grasp the idea?
A sticky situation.
I feel it in my bones.
One step at a time.

Auditory Digital Metaphors

Makes Sense.
Without a doubt.
I can't figure it out.
Let me process this.

Communication Assessment

For each of the following statements, please assign a number to every phrase. Use the following system to indicate your preferences:

1. Least descriptive of you.
2. Next best description.
3. Next best description.
4. Best description of you.

If you are having trouble deciding, select the first thought that comes to mind.

Answer these questions:

1. When vacationing at the beach, the first thing that makes me glad to be there is:
   A. __ The feel of the cool sand, the warm sun or the fresh breeze on my face.
   B. __ The roar of the waves, the whistling wind or the sound of the birds in the distance.
   C. __ This is the type of vacation that makes sense or the cost is reasonable.
   D. __ The scenery, the bright sun, and the blue water.
2. When overwhelmed, I find it helps if:
   A. __ I can see the big picture.
   B. __ I can hear what's going on.
   C. __ I can get in touch with what is happening.
   D. __ I make sense of things in my head.
3. When given an assignment at work, it is easier to carry out if:
   A. __ I can picture what is required.
   B. __ I have a feeling for what is required.
   C. __ I have an understanding of what is required.
   D. __ I have tuned into what's required.

4. I find it easier to follow a presentation if:

A. __ I feel in touch with the presenter and the material is in my grasp.
B. __ There is a visual display so that I can visualize the concepts.
C. __ The presentation is based on facts and figures ad is logically presented.
D. __ The presenter speaks clearly with varying tonality or uses sound to emphasize the message.

5. When buying a car, I make my decision on:

A. __ The purchase price, gas mileage, safety features, etc.
B. __ How comfortable the seats are or the feeling I get when I test drive it.
C. __ The color, styling or how I look in it.
D. __ The sound of the engine or stereo system or how quiet it rides.

6. I communicate my thoughts through:

A. __ My tone of voice.
B. __ My words.
C. __ My appearance.
D. __ My feelings.

7. When I am anxious, the first thing that happens is:

A. __ Things begin to sound different.
B. __ Things begin to feel different.
C. __ Things begin to look different.
D. __ Things begin to not make sense.

8. During a discussion, I am most often influenced by:
   A. __ The other person's logic.
   B. __ The other person's tone of voice.
   C. __ The energy I feel from the other person.
   D. __Seeing the other person's body language or being able to picture their viewpoint

9. I assess how well I am doing at work based on:
   A. __ My understanding of what needs to be done.
   B. __ How I see myself making progress.
   C. __ How things sound.
   D. __How satisfied I feel.

10. One of my strengths is my ability to:
   A. __ See what needs to be done.
   B. __ Make sense of new facts and data.
   C. __ Here what sounds right.
   D. __ Get in touch with my feelings

11. I enjoy:
   A. __ Choosing a piece of music to listen to.
   B. __ Making a logical, compelling point.
   C. __ Choosing clothes that are comfortable.
   D. __ Choosing clothes the look good.

12: If you agree with someone, you are more likely to say:
   A. __ That feels right.
   B. __ That looks right.
   C. __ That sounds right.
   D. __ That makes sense.

Circle your answers below:

Question Number	Visual	Auditory	Kinesthetic	Digital
1	D	B	A	C
2	A	B	C	D
3	A	D	B	C
4	B	D	A	C
5	C	D	B	A
6	C	A	D	B
7	C	A	B	D
8	D	B	C	A
9	B	C	D	A
10	A	C	D	B
11	D	A	C	B
12	B	C	A	D
Total	V =	A =	K =	D =

Add the numbers in each column. Compare the totaled scores to determine your relative preference for each of the four major representational systems. The higher the score, the higher your preference

Eye Accessing Cues

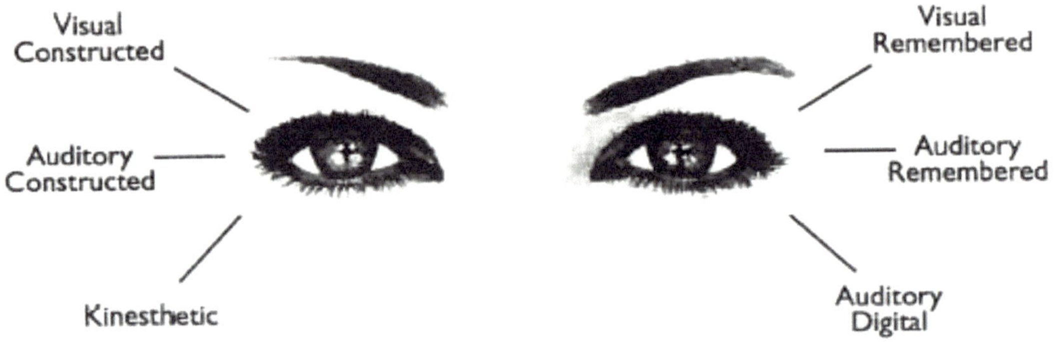

Examples:

Visual Remembered

What is the color of the shirt you wore yesterday?

Which of your friends has the shortest hair?

Visual Constructed

What would your room look like if it were painted yellow with big purple circles?

Can you imagine the top half of a tiger on the bottom half of an elephant?

Auditory Remembered

What does your best friend's voice sound like?

Which is louder, your door bell or your telephone?

Auditory Constructed

What will your voice sound like in 10 years?

What would it sound like if you played your two favorite pieces of music at the same time?

Auditory Digital

What is something you continually tell yourself?

What are your thoughts about this article?

Kinesthetic

What does it feel like to walk barefoot on a cool sandy beach?

What does it feel like when you rub your fingers on sandpaper?

Eye Accessing Cues -The Easy Way

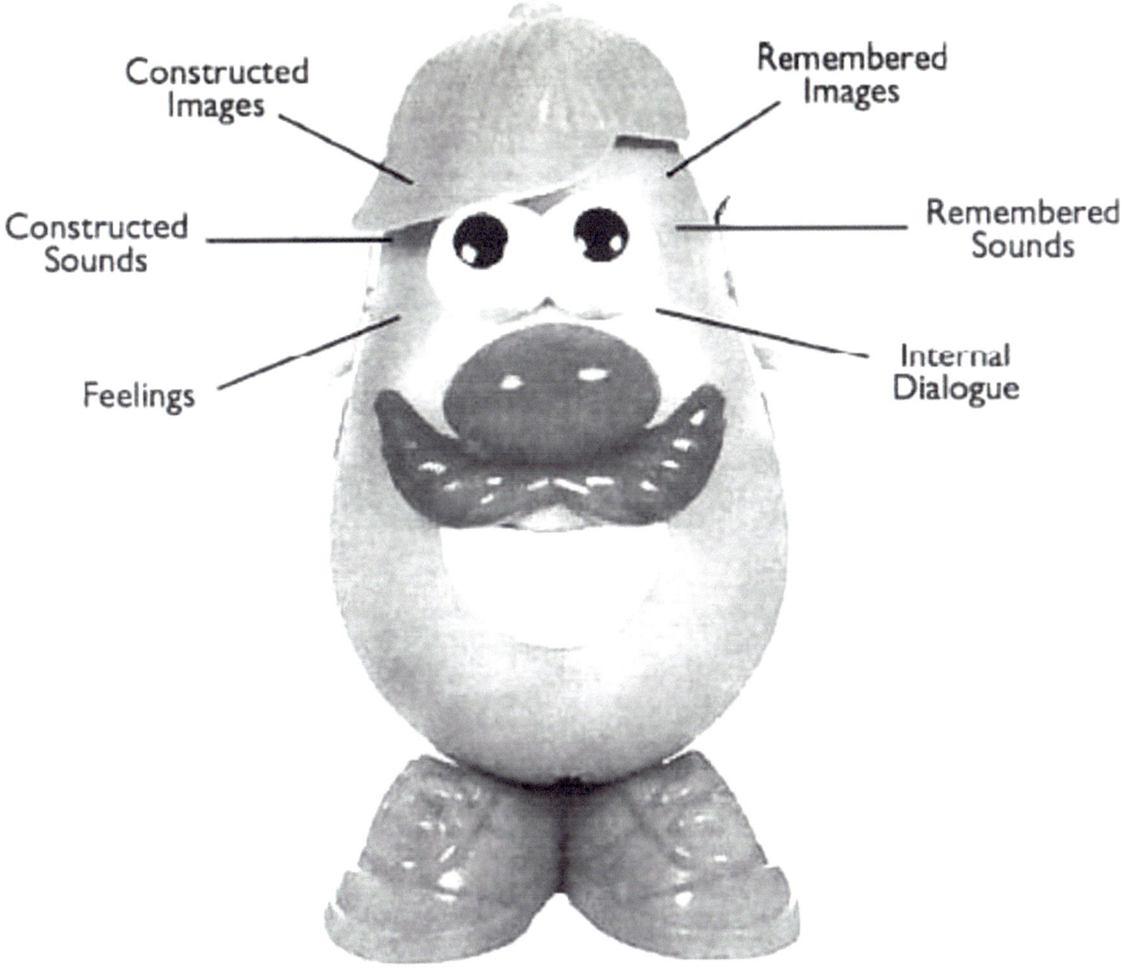

Note: It's easy to remember that the eye cues indicate auditory (constructed or remembered) as they are on the same horizontal plane as the individuals ears.

Questions to Detect Eye Patterns

V^R "What color was the room you grew up in?"

V^C "Imagine your room if it were blue."

A^M "What was the very last thing I said?"

A^C "Imagine what I just said with Donald Duck's voice."

K "Imagine what it feels like to touch a wet rug."

A_O Recite the pledge of Allegiance to yourself."

MENTALISM:

1. In a moment, I'm going to ask you to think of one of three things:
   a. The most beautiful sunset you've ever seen
   b. Your favorite song
   c. How it feels to slip into a nice hot bath or Jacuzzi

Don't tell me which one. Just concentrate on one now…

How Do We Communicate?

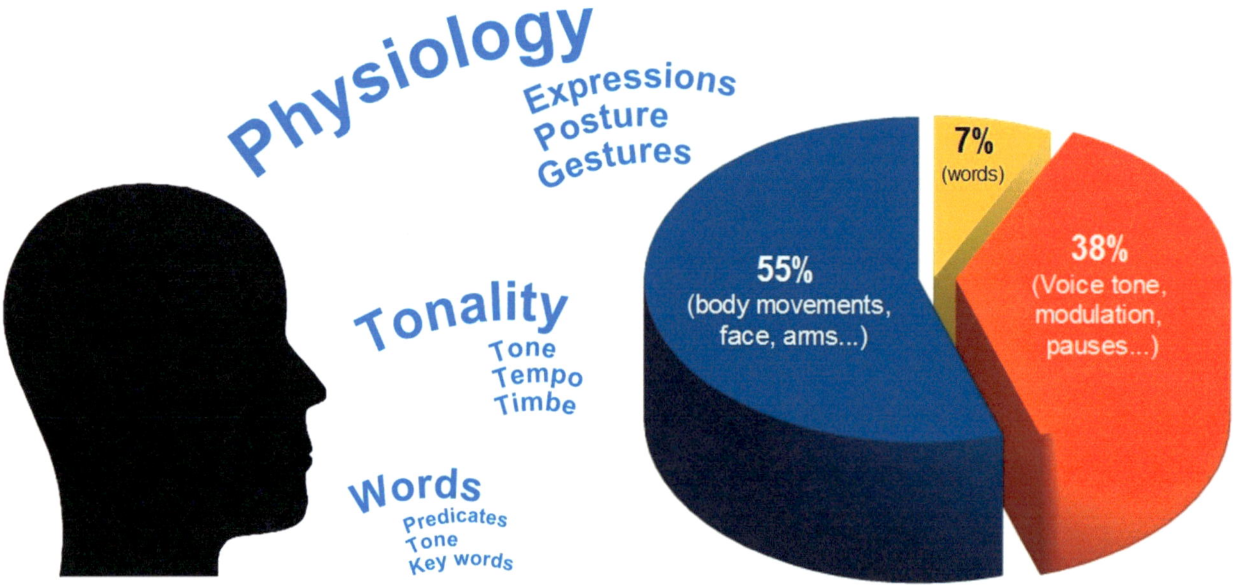

Communication is:

7% Words | **38%** Tonality | **55%** Physiology

Building Rapport

Building rapport is built on a process of responsiveness, not necessarily "liking." Rapport is established by Mirroring and Matching another person.

Mirroring and Matching is subtly modeling behaviors of the person we are communicating with to build natural rapport.

Physiology

- ~ Posture
- ~ Hand Gestures
- ~ Facial Expressions
- ~ Spinal Alignment
- ~ Head Tilt
- ~ Blinking
- ~ Breathing Rate (Watch the shoulders & location of breath)
- ~ Energy Level

Tonality

- ~ Tone (Pitch)
- ~ Tempo (Speed)
- ~ Timbre (Quality)
- ~ Volume (Loudness/Quietness)

Words

- ~ Predicates
- ~ Key Words
- ~ Common Experiences
- ~ Content Chunk (Amount of words used)

When you are fully mirroring and matching, you will be sitting with the same posture of the person you are communicating with, using the same types of gestures, speaking at a similar speed, volume and tone, and breathing at the same rate as the other person. Notice what it feels like when you have reached this level of rapport.

11 Points of Contact to Build Rapport

1. Marketing Email/Social Media/Mailer
2. New Patient Call
3. Confirmation Call
4. Walking Into Reception Area
5. Meeting Front Office Team
6. Hand Off To Hygienist/Assistant
7. Hand Off To Doctor
8. Hand Off To Treatment Coordinator
9. Email/Text Asking For A Review
10. Treatment Care Call
11. Welcome Letter

Three Communication Types

Internal Communication - How well you communicate with yourself

External Communication - How well you communicate with others

Persuasion - How well you influence yourself and others

How Well do you Currently Control Your Emotional State?

As your internal communication improves, you will begin to operate more effectively. You will be able to control your emotional state, motivate yourself effectively and find your way to greater success in most areas of your life.

Exercise

Imagine or remember a time that an event, this could be someone said something or something, or something happened and you reacted emotionally to that person or thing.

- How long have you reacted that way?
- Would you like to learn to react differently?
- What would be different if you did?

Patient Interview

The Object of the Patient Interview:

~ To establish immediate rapport
~ To establish trust and likeability
~ To understand our patient's model of the world and what they value
~ To discover how our patient processes information through their senses
~ To determine our patient's buying strategies

How do we discover what is important to our patients? Smile Questionnaire.

1. ____.

2. ____.

3. ____.

4. ____.

5. ____.

Clarification Of Responses Using Key Words: Creating An Emotional Connection

~ What I hear you saying is………..Tell me more about that…

~ What else?

~ What will that do for you?

~ How long have you been dealing with this pain/discomfort?

~ What have you not been able to do because of this?

~ What will you finally be able to do once we have fixed this? What will that do for you?

~ So, is it fair to say, that it's important for you to have this fixed?

~ What stops you from…..

~ What would happen if……..(Creating Possibility)

Treatment Planning

Treatment Planning: The Process

Do you get frustrated when patients tell you "Let me think about it"?

Do you feel disappointed when your patients choose the least expensive procedures?

Have you ever wondered why a patient said "No" to your treatment when you just had such a great conversation with them?

What is a Successfully closed treatment case?

1. ____.

2. ____.

3. ____.

4. ____.

5. ____.

6. ____.

People do not buy solutions to problems they do not think they have. In dentistry, when diagnosing, teams tend to go straight from the problem to the solution. In turn, this approach results in less than a 33% treatment acceptance rate.

33% of your patients will say "Yes" to your diagnosis

33% of your patients will say "No" to your diagnosis

33% of your patients will say "Maybe" to your diagnosis

Filters

We listen to people through a sea of opinions (our filters) instead of listening to what they truly say and how they are responding to our actions. These are filters that always exist with us and are manifested through our culture, experiences, surroundings, etc. They are a fundamental set of assumptions we "create" about others. Assumptions that are not recognized as assumptions, but as *Truth*.

Filters are that little internal voice that keeps talking to us all throughout the day. It tells us:

What is right / What is wrong

This should happen / This should not happen

This is good / This is bad

What is this?

Our listening becomes so automatic that we do not realize we are listening to others through OUR personal filters, interpretations and opinions.

Example:

- He is always a difficult patient
- She can't afford a crown
- He always tries to get a discount

Become aware of your listening and speaking filters with every conversation. Distinguish YOUR filter from what is being said by others. Be aware and 100% responsible for how you define another's beliefs.

The Power Of Yes Questions

Why Do We Start Our Conversation With "Yes" Questions?

____

____

____

What Are Examples Of "Yes" Questions

____

____

____

Starting The "Yes" Process with The End Result In Mind

Eight-Step Process to Build Rapport with Every Patient:

1. Establish Rapport
2. Understand Your Patient's Values
3. Discover How Your Patient Processes Information
4. Determine Your Patient's Buying Strategies
5. Link the Need or Value to Your Product/Service

6. Build Authority

7: Leverage Social Proof

8. Close

1. Rapport: Rapport is the most important tool in unconscious human interactions. It is being in sync with someone. Being on the same wavelength.

- ***Mirroring and Matching**:* Matching someone's body language (gestures), tone of voice, words and cadence of voice. You *mirror* the other person. This is a must when creating a first impression with anyone. This naturally allows you to connect quickly with your patient and is the first step in influencing them. Remember, we *like* people *like* us!

2. Understanding Your Patient's Values*:* By asking effective questions, you can discover what they value about their overall health, not just their teeth. As you discover their values, you also learn the rules they hold that support those values. Begin with questions:

1. "*What is the most important thing we can do for you today?*" (Value)

2. "*What does ____________ mean to you*?" (Rules) (Remember to never assume you understand because their rules are different than yours)

OR

1. Doctor: "*What is most important to you in your relationship with a dentist?*"

   Patient*: "That he respects me." (Value)*

2. Doctor*: "What would have to happen in order for you to know that you are respected?"*

   Patient*: "Being on time. Not talking down to me. Being a good listener. Allowing me to participate in making the final decision" (Rules)*

OR

"What is most important to you in your relationship with your dental practice?"

"What do you like most about your teeth?"

"What is most important to you about your teeth?"

"What did you like most about your last dental office?"

3. Discover How Your Patient Processes Information: We get information about the world through our five senses. We tend to rely more on one or two versus all of them. You and your team want to learn what modality your patient is most comfortable with. Visual, Auditory, Kinesthetic, Auditory Digital.

- **Visual Patients**: Speak more quickly. They are attracted to pictures, models, imaging, drawings, intraoral pictures, x-rays, visual descriptions and visual words. When they think about something, they look up with their eyes. Use words like *see, look, focus, clear, envision*. Ask them if they can picture what this will look like? *Can you see how this treatment will benefit you? Is that clear to you?*
- **Auditory Patients**: Love to talk and be listened to. They love verbal communication. They want explanations. They are more social and are affected by auditory words. These patients have a tendency to lose interest in overuse of visual demonstrations. When they think about something, they look laterally towards the ears. Use words like hear, listen, sound. Use phrases like *let's talk about your treatment plan, I hear what you are saying, let's fine-tune your appointments, that sounds great, does that sound good to you?*

- **Kinesthetic Patients**: Are emotionally driven. They are responsive to gentle touching. They have low interest in intraoral pictures. They often speak more slowly, and are more sensitive to temperature and pressure. When they think about something, they look down to the right. Use words like *feel, touch, solid*. And, use phrases such as *let's get a handle on this, can you feel how this treatment plan will provide you with long-term health? I know we can firm up appointments for you to fit your schedule, can you get in touch with this treatment plan?*

- **Auditory Digital**: Digitals speak using words that are not related to their senses and they like to think things through before making a decision. They understand by steps, procedures and sequences. When they think, they look down to the left. Use phrases such as *makes sense, figure it out, that's logical, let me process this, I can't figure this out, does this treatment make sense to you? Do you understand the steps we will be taking?*

4. Patient Buying Strategies: Buying strategies re the general, pervasive, habitual patterns we use in our language patterns and body language to determine how we think, react and behave.

- **Towards vs. Away**: A person's attention is either directed *towards* what they want or a*way* from what they don't want. This helps you understand if a patient is more drawn to the benefits of something or resistant based on the consequences. What compels them to take action, pleasure or pain? For example:

  Doctor: *"What is most important to you about your teeth?"*

  Patient*: "I want to keep my teeth." (Benefits)*

  Patient*: "I don't want to lose my teeth." (Consequences)*

The result is the same but the language to get to the result is different.

Are the following questions geared towards a patient who values benefits or consequences?

Doctor: *"The benefits to you of this treatment are ...."*

Doctor: "By accepting this treatment you avoid ...."

Doctor: "In order for you to get healthy, you must (Protocol)."

Doctor: "To avoid losing your teeth, you must (Protocol)."

- **Big Picture vs. Detail**: Define if a patient is a big picture or detail person.

  Doctor: *"When I explain this treatment plan to you, would you like the big picture or the details?"*

Doctor Big Picture Presentation: *"The treatment I recommend involves three crowns and two fillings. It will take two visits and can be completed in three weeks. You said earlier, you are leaving town next month and if it were me, I would want to get those done immediately because (EM & Modality)"*

Doctor Detail Presentation: *"I highly recommend a crown on #7 because .... And a similar crown on #28 because .... We do a crown by first removing the cracked and decayed tooth structure. You said earlier, you are leaving town next month and if it were me, I would want to get those done immediately because (EM & Modality)"*

If you give this level of detail to a big picture person, they will become anxious and distracted. Their eyes will glaze over and they will more than likely not accept treatment. If you give too big a picture to a detail person, they will feel short-changed and not cared for.

5. Link Need with Consequence, then Solutions

Create a story/scenario linking their consequence to their need then linking it to your solution. (Example: Cracked tooth/Holidays)

6. Authority:

People tend to trust and obey confident authority figures because they believe their knowledge is superior.

7. Social Proof:

People will do things they see other people doing. Most people will look for guidance when they are uncertain about making decisions and taking action.

- Provide testimonials
- Provide pictures
- Stories of successful cases
- Stories of consequence

8. Close—Ask for It

Back Office Clinicians, overcome ALL objections before handing the patient off to the treatment coordinator. If a patient says they want to think about it, ask their spouse, check their schedule, you have not overcome their objections and you want to dig deeper and ask more questions ("What is holding you back").

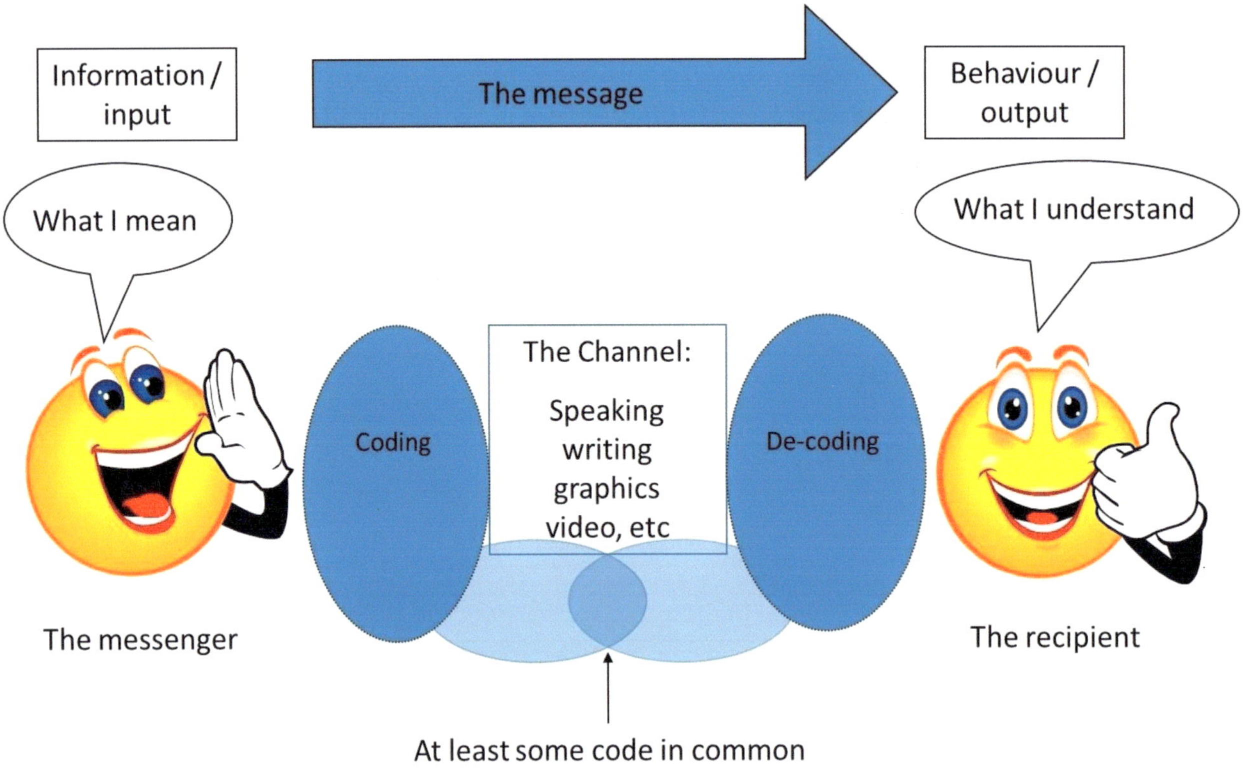

Maximizing vs. Minimizing Words

The ability to communicate effectively and confidently has a dramatic effect on our ability to serve our patients properly.

Minimizing Words

Little
A little bit
Tiny
Brief
To Be honest with you
I think
This is just my opinion, but…
This may not be relevant, but…
I *just*…… want, think, feel, vs. I want you to know
Does that make sense?
Apologizing before starting a sentence
Ummmmm
What I'm trying to say is
I'll try
Basically
You know
I'm a little bit …. concerned
I don't know vs. I'm going to do some research on that

Maximizing Your Diagnosis

A cavity vs. A small cavity

A crack vs. A small crack

It is imperative vs. I think

I want you to get in my schedule vs. When are you available to come in

Active periodontal infection vs. gum inflammation

Periodontal Therapy vs. Deep cleaning, scaling, root planning, quad scaling

Permanent bone damage vs. bone loss

Daily disease control vs. Home care

Closely monitored interval vs. 6-week, 3-month appointment

Optimal clinical results vs. reduce pocket depth

Disease remission vs. reduce infection

Insurance assistance vs. insurance coverage (which implies complete)

RDH Magazine

Look, Listen, Notice, Pay Attention

Treatment Planning: Putting It All Together

Problem: ____

Consequences: ____

Emotional Motivators: ____________________________________

Solution: ____

Example: Crown

Problem: ____

____

Consequences: ____

____

____

____

____

Emotional Motivators: ____________________________________

____

____

____

Solution: ____

____

____

____

____

Call to Action Statement: ______________________________

____

____

____

____

Possible Objection:

____

____

____

Complaints and Objections: How To Handle Them

Overcoming patients' objections is easily handled by reframing their thought process. Remember, always *acknowledge* and *agree* with a patient's concerns so you open their thought process to new possibilities.

Money-Related

I don't have the money

- What if you did have the money to *invest in this treatment*, where would it have come from?
- If we could reduce the payment down to something you could afford, would you schedule your treatment? *[Talk payment plan options]*
- What is the most you can afford? What number would make it achievable? ($250) Great, here's how I can help you. Put the $250 down now and we can run $xxx payments each month for 12 months.

  [If they object, tie it to the payment, not the deposit.]

I'm out of work

- That's awesome! Because you have something other people don't – time. Many people who want to get their treatment don't because they're **in** work! You have the perfect opportunity.

My credit cards are maxed

- I used to think that was a real problem too, but one of our patients actually told me that if you have a good reason –especially an investment like this – they'll extend your credit line. Lots of our patients do this so they have the payment flexibility.
- We also have a flexible payment plan. This will allow you to get started right now and pay it off over time. How does that sound?

Your prices are more expensive than other offices

- Yes, some offices are *cheaper* than ours, but there are much more important things to consider than price, aren't there?
- If you were going to have brain surgery, you wouldn't want to pick the cheapest surgeon who went through the minimum amount of training at the cheapest school, would you? Of course not! [Command tonality- lower voice] It just makes sense to make the best investment in yourself you can, so you get the healthiest teeth/mouth, doesn't it? [Command tonality- lower voice]

I'll schedule later, or I'll think about it, I'm just not ready

- Ask, "What is it that keeps you from scheduling today?" *[Note: If they are a maybe, keep reframing and handling objections until you get a yes or a no.]*

Top Dental Procedures **and The Consequence Of No Treatment**

Procedure: ____

Cause of Problem: ____

Consequences of Not Treating: _______________________________

____

Solution: ____

____

Procedure: ____

Cause of Problem: ____

Consequences of Not Treating: _______________________________

____

Solution: ____

____

Procedure: ____

Cause of Problem: ____

Consequences of Not Treating: ________________________________

____

Solution: ____

____

Procedure: ____

Cause of Problem: ____

Consequences of Not Treating: ________________________________

____

Solution: ____

____

Procedure: ____

Cause of Problem: ____

Consequences of Not Treating: ________________________________

____

Solution: ____

____

Procedure: ____

Cause of Problem: ____

Consequences of Not Treating: _______________________________

____

Solution: ____

____

Procedure: ____

Cause of Problem: ____

Consequences of Not Treating: _______________________________

____

Solution: ____

____

Procedure: ______________________________________

Cause of Problem: __________________________________

Consequences of Not Treating: _______________________

____

Solution: ____

____

Procedure: ______________________________________

Cause of Problem: __________________________________

Consequences of Not Treating: _______________________

____

Solution: ____

____

Nine Pillars of Influence

1. Contrast

Contrast highlights the differences between two or more options

Providing the proper contrast can tip the balance in your favor

Example: Let's say a salesman wanted to sell you a $5,000 TV. Would you be more inclined to buy that TV if he first showed you a $500 TV, or if he first showed you a $10,000 TV? Most people will be turned off by a second price that is 10x more than the first price, no matter how good it is. However, in contrast to $10,000, the target price of $500 seems more "reasonable" being only 50%.

2. Reciprocation

Our society is set up in such a way that if you give someone something, they feel compelled to reciprocate.

This is so deeply ingrained that often people will do what they don't want to do simply because they feel a deep need to reciprocate.

Example: Hare Krishnas, Easter Seals

3. Commitment and Consistency

The subconscious mind will do everything in its power to remain consistent with commitments we have made.

There is a trait that runs very deep in human behavior, and that is the need to be consistent.

Once people have made a commitment to a statement, ideal or agreement, they will do everything in their power to remain consistent with that decision; often to levels that appear silly to impartial observers and sometimes to their own detriment.

Example: Micro commitments, buyer consistency

4. Social Proof

The more people doing something; the more everybody else will want to do it too.

Our subconscious mind likes to take the path of least resistance.

One way to do that is to generalize things by looking at peers and society and determine social norms. Rather than reasoning out whether or not something makes sense, we often place our judgment on whatever the masses are doing.

Example: Testimonials, photos of patients, schedule full

"Nothing draws a crowd like a crowd" - P. T. Barnum

5. Liking (Rapport)

People like people who are like them.

It is built into our human neurology that we tend to like and trust people whoa re like ourselves.

Example: Behaviors, language, common interests, associations, appearances

6. Authority

People will suspend their own judgment or belief in exchange for those of an authority figure.

When a person of sufficient authority speaks, we simply accept their suggestions without critical thought.

Example: Degrees, certifications, media appearances, endorsements from authority figures

7. Scarcity and Take Aways

People tend to want what they can't have. Scarcity creates desire and motivation.

In many studies, it has been proven that products and services that are scarce are generally more "in demand" than if they were not scarce.

Example: Early-Bird specials, only 5 left in stock, 50% off today only

8. Perceived Value

People will go to greater lengths to get something with a higher perceived value.

Perceived value is the ultimate use to create a value for what you have to offer.

Many people believe "expensive = good"

The trick, and it takes some experimentation, is to find the balance between being expensive enough to create perceived value, but not so expensive that you lose the majority of your potentially interested patients.

Examples: High prices, exclusivity, qualification, endorsement titles (Diamond, Platinum)

9. Motivation Direction

People are usually motivated away form pain/consequences or toward pleasure/rewards and typically a combination of both depending on the situation.

Different things motivate different people. While one person may be more motivated to take action by the offer of a bonus, like a trip to Hawaii; another person won't be motivated until their job is on the line

Tips to Effective Treatment Planning

~ Use patient's name 5 times especially when discussing emotional motivators, consequences, solutions and guiding patient to schedule

~ Speak patient, not clinical: Keep the dental terminology to a minimum

~ Treatment is ALWAYS diagnosed based on Ideal Care instead of insurance and fees (Filters)

~ Use maximizing words when discussing consequences and minimizing words when discussing solutions

~ Create Urgency: "I want you to get on my schedule in the next week. Do you prefer morning or afternoon? Assistant/hygienist, what is our next available morning for (patient)?"

~ Be concise and to the point, quickly

~ Patients only hear **20%** of what you say when you are *talking to them* and they hear **100%** of what you say when you are *talking about them* to another person. This is why effective hand offs are essential

~ Provide your patient every resource they need to make a decision

~ When complaints/objections arise, always acknowledge and agree

7 Principles for Case Acceptance Success

1. Always know your Outcome for every patient interaction

2. Take all necessary Action to prepare and attain outcome

3. Monitor your Results and Feedback

4. Be Open and Flexible to changing your Behavior based on the feedback you receive

5. Always focus on Excellence instead of perfection

6. Be Integrity

7. Speak and act with Gratitude

Treatment Plan Checklist

1. Review treatment with patient
2. Provide educational video if not done in treatment room
3. Ask patient if they understand all treatment needed
4. Review fees & make financial arrangements
5. Schedule appointment
6. Ask for scheduling deposit
7. Provide folder including: Treatment plan, picture of tooth, financial arrangements, healthy mouth overview, philosophy of practice, brochure of procedure, consequences sheet, appointment card
8. Check out: Provide walkout statement & give line by line explanation
9. Email video with brief note

Treatment Plan Folder Includes:

Treatment Plan

Financial Arrangements

Appointment card

Copies of x-rays with areas circled by doctors

Healthy Mouth Baseline

Brochures/Informationals

Business Card

Membership Program Brochure

(If perio) print colored copy of perio charting to show pockets & bleeding points

The Handoff

The Patient Hand Off is how you successfully transition your patient from one team member to another. Consistently utilizing this transfer throughout the entire appointment will ensure your patient experiences the highest level of service.

Acknowledging and listening to your patients is the key to successfully transferring your patients! The highest honor you can give your patients is to listen to them without interruption. Slow down and listen to your patients. Repeat, verbatim everything they say, so they feel as if they have been heard. Take notes to ensure you are repeating their keywords, emotions and concerns accurately.

Take the time to really "tune in" to your patients. Ask about birthdays, anniversaries, vacations, reunions, weddings, pregnancies, etc. Every patient has a story, but won't necessarily volunteer it. So, you have to find out what it is. Use these questions to get to know every new patient and modify them for existing patients:

- *Tell me about some of the dental treatment you have had in the past. Can you tell me more about that? Why was that treatment done?*
- *How long has it been since you have had any dental work?*
- *What has kept you away for so long? (fears!!!) Do you have any missing teeth? Was anything ever suggested to replace them?*
- *Are there any stains or spots on your teeth that you are worried about?*
- *Anything else about how your teeth look that concerns you?*
- *How would you rate the appearance of your teeth on a scale of 1-10? Why a seven? What would make it a 10?*
- *Why did you leave your last dentist? What did you like most about your last dentist? What did you like least about your last dentist?*
- *I know this is a lot of questions, but we hope you will become a patient of this practice for many years. So we want to make sure we give you just what you want and just what you need.*

When you hand the patient off to the next team member, you should give an explanation to the next team member about:

- Patient's concerns
- Any significant personal information
- What has been completed
- What needs to be completed

People only hear **20%** of what you say when you talk directly to them however; they hear **100%** of what you say when you talk ABOUT them to another person.

The Patient Hand Off Means **Repeat, Repeat, Repeat!**

Examples of Patient Hand Off

Front office to Clinical Team: Hi Tiffany, this is Melanie and she is visiting our office for the first time! John Smith is a good friend of hers and he referred her to our office! Melanie has a wedding coming up in June so she is really excited and wants to have Doctor take a look at a couple of her front teeth as well as learn more about tooth whitening! She also has a bit of sensitivity in her lower gums.

Melanie, Tiffany is fantastic and our expert and she will take great care of you today! Have a great visit!

<u>Clinical Team to Doctor:</u> Hi Dr. Jones, this is Melanie. Melanie is visiting us for the first time. She works with John Smith at Mesa Community College. He recommended she come and see you before her wedding in June. She really wants to fix her front, bottom teeth and do some teeth whitening before the wedding parties start. We have done a full set of x-rays and pictures. She is having a bit of sensitivity in her gums. Melanie is also taking _________ medication and has a history of diabetes. I explained to Melanie how her diabetes affects her gingivitis. I have also shown Melanie the picture of the crack on her lower left tooth and discussed the possibility of wanting a crown to protect the tooth.

Melanie, this is Dr. Jones, he is going to take great care of you and make sure you smile looks beautiful for your wedding!

<u>Doctor to Patient:</u> (Sit down by patient's knees, look patient in the eyes, smile, maintain a confident posture.) Hi Melanie, I am Dr. Jones. It is great to meet you! So, John Smith recommended you come see me? John is such a great patient; we really like him. Tiffany tells me you are getting married in June! That is really exciting. Well, let's get you all taken care of so you have the smile you want for your wedding. Tell me about the sensitivity you are feeling. (Do exam, review x-rays/pictures)

Melanie, Tiffany is correct. You have a crack in your lower left tooth (show picture) and a crack ignored turns into a broken tooth causing possible root canal, extraction and an implant. In my experience, these things happen at the worst times, like when you are trying to enjoy your wedding parties! Let's keep this simple and protect you and your tooth and place a crown on your tooth to maintain its structure. You don't want to be dealing with pain and all those appointments from a broken tooth around your wedding, do you (command lower tone)? I agree. Melanie, I want you to get in my schedule immediately so we can take care of you before your tooth breaks. Do you prefer mornings or afternoons?

Clinical Team to Treatment Coordinator: Hi Theresa, this is Melanie and she has a big day coming up in June! She is getting married and we are going to do some veneers and teeth whitening so she will have a beautiful smile. We also found a crack on her lower left tooth and have scheduled her this Thursday at 10:00am to get that taken care of immediately before it cracks. We have prioritized her treatment for you.

Melanie, welcome to our practice and call if you need anything. You did a great job. Theresa is going to take great care of you! See you in a few days!

Treatment Coordinator to Patient: (Print out treatment plan and get side-by-side with your patient whether standing or sitting) Melanie, Doctor explained to you the importance of getting your cracked tooth taken care of now so you can enjoy your time with your family and friends and all the fun things you will be doing before your wedding! You are making a good decision to get your health taken care of now. Your investment will be _______. How would you like to pay for that? (Stay quiet and give your patient a moment to figure out how to pay for it)

Your patients will probably never see or know the efforts you and your team made on their behalf (team meetings, chart reviews, morning huddles), but they will always remember how your dental experience made them feel. Perfect your hand-offs and create happy patients and future referrals!

Hand Off Quick List

P/C/EM/S:

Problem

Consequences

Emotional Motivator – Time, Pain, Money

Solution

Example:

> "I want you to get on my schedule this week because (lists 3 consequences of not taking action now) and those are going to be more painful (kinesthetic), cost you more money (Logical) and require more appointments (Time)."

Hygiene

5-Star Preventative Therapy

Think about the finest restaurant you've ever enjoyed, a restaurant where you were so delighted with the meal, the setting, and the service that the final tab didn't much concern you. You know that restaurant – the one you measure all other restaurants against. The one you recommend to absolutely everybody.

Did the waiter smile, greet you, hold your chair, and introduce himself? Did she wait for you to decide what you wanted or did she make recommendations about the menu, based on what you were celebrating or what was particularly tasty? Did he persuade you to order dessert even though you were fully stuffed? Did she recommend the perfect wine to pair with your food?

In the restaurant setting, the waiter is the first point of culinary contact between the chef and the diner. He is **THE source of information about the menu**. He can, quite literally, make or break the restaurant's reputation and profitability.

In your practice, the first point of medical contact your patients see during their visit, **your hygienist is THE source of information regarding your practice's "menu" of preventative services**. Your hygienist can, quite literally, make or break your practice's reputation and profitability.

Does your hygienist smile, greet patients by name, introduce himself or herself, get to know the patient and make sure the patient is comfortable?

Does your hygienist wait for the patient to decide what he or she wants, or does the hygienist **actively recommend services based on what patients need, after determining what they want**?

The 5-Star Hygienist can add over $110,000 per year to your practice by taking an active role in recommending three simple, inexpensive treatments: fluoride, sealant, and de-sensitizing agent.

But first, you have to know your own numbers.

Know Your Numbers: How to Measure your Effectiveness as a Preventative Therapist

Does your hygienist actively recommend fluoride, sealants, and de-sensitizing agents? How many patients accept? How many decline?

How many of your hygiene patients accept recommended fluoride treatments? The national average is fewer than 20 per cent.

How many of your patients accept sealants? Research indicates that everyone has a 95 percent chance of developing caries in the cracks and fissures of their teeth. The ADA recommends sealants as the treatment of choice for patients over 40 due to changing health concerns in that age group.

How many of your patients accept desensitizing agents? More than 85 per cent of adults report tooth sensitivity, and there are several bonding agents that seal and protect the sensitive Class V area revealed by recession.

If your hygienist does NOT have **a fluoride acceptance rate of 80 per cent or more**, if fewer than **four patients accept sealants every day**, and if your **acceptance rate for de-sensitizing agents is less than 80 per cent**, you have some work to do. Your hygienist is quite literally leaving money on the table, and you are not serving your patients to the best of your ability.

Let's fix those numbers, by examining how your hygienist communicates with patients, and the best ways to communicate to be a 5-Star Preventative Therapist.

How to Communicate with Patients to Deliver 5-Star Preventative Therapy

The more you educate your patients and involve them in the decision-making, the higher your acceptance rate will be.

During Tissue Health Assessments:

Begin every single **Tissue Health Assessment** with a conversation that educates your patient about what you're looking for. That way, your recommendations will make sense to them. Here's an example of how to set up your patient to listen:

> *"I am going to check your tissue for infection. This will help us detect any possible problems or disease in your gums. You will hear me saying a series of numbers for each tooth and I am going to record the findings for you. A 1-3 means that your tissue is healthy. A 4 means infection is present and 5 or higher indicates that the infection has already spread to the bone. Pay attention and count how many times you hear a "4" or higher called out. I am also going to document your bleeding points and areas of inflammation."*

As you go through the exam, recording the numbers aloud, whenever they hear a 4 or a 5, they will become slightly anxious, and begin to wonder, "*"What do I need to do to fix that?"*

At the end of the exam, show them the data. Print out a color copy of their perio exam chart, and present it to them, pointing out the problems you found.

The patient will now rely on you to offer a solution – a "recommendation from the menu," if you will, instead of perceiving your suggestion as an attempt to "sell" them something they don't know they need.

How to Recommend Fluoride Treatment

When presenting the option of a **fluoride treatment**, many hygienists make the assumption (out loud) that "insurance probably won't pay for it," thus shooting themselves in the foot and providing an excuse for the patient to decline.

Instead, use language like this to improve your fluoride acceptance percentage and help your patients see the value of investing in topically applied fluoride:

> *"Here is why fluoride would be good for you today."*

(Share with your patient specific reasons why fluoride will benefit them. For example, fluoride can help protect areas like exposed root surfaces, dry mouth, crown margins, large fillings, or lots of restorations. Your patient has spent time and money rebuilding their mouth, and fluoride will help prevent recurrent decay and failure in their dental work.)

> *"The bad news is that insurance won't help with you the cost. But the good news is the topical application of fluoride is affordable and it's only $25. That is a small price to pay against having to replace crowns and restorations in the not-too-distant future."*

Or...

> *"You might not be aware of it, but new research shows that if we do a fluoride varnish every time we polish your teeth, we can reduce future cavities by as much as 75%. Earlier you mentioned that you were frustrated with always having problems with your teeth. Let's turn that around. Fluoride varnish can help you do that."*

How to Recommend Sealants

A few years ago, we wouldn't have thought to do sealants on an adult. But with the challenges we are seeing in patients, medications that cause xerostomia and other risk factors, coupled with the enhancement of technology, we are able to make better determinations about which teeth are the best candidates for sealants.

In fact, prosthodontists are teaching that sealants should be the treatment of choice for anyone over the age of 40, due to increasing changes in health conditions as people age. **Educate** your patients using these facts:

"I'm going to recommend we apply a sealant today. Here's why:

1. *Current research tells us that everyone has a **95%** chance of caries in the pits and fissures of their teeth if we don't use sealants."*
2. *We know that sealants stop early stage cavities and incipient decay. It's amazing, but the research shows that if you apply a sealant at each cleaning, and monitor and maintain it, you can reduce decay by as much as 74% over a 15-year period.*
3. *The detection technology and materials available to us now are of much higher quality than they used to be, so we can monitor and track this reduction."*

Then close by saying this:

"The American Dental Association standard of care is to recommend sealants on ALL posterior teeth (or for all patients over 40) NOT just those that insurance will pay for. But the cost is very minimal, at $35, especially when you compare it to the expense of dealing with possible future decay and the need for more crowns or other restorative work."

When you talk about the value of sealants, emphasize the value of same-day sealants. Your patients want fast, convenient service, and the more often you can provide it, the more successful you will be.

How to Recommend De-Sensitizing Agents

The opportunity to help patients relieve pain and alleviate sensitivity is enormous. After all, **over 80% of the adult population suffers from sensitive teeth, affecting 45 million people** in the United States.

Think about it. How many of **your** patients would benefit from desensitizing agents? How many of them would sincerely appreciate your solving this problem?

When you recommend a desensitizing agent in the right way, **you can achieve acceptance rates of up to 89%**. Here's the script we use:

> *"We have an exciting new service that can help immediately remove the pain and discomfort from your sensitive tooth. It will also protect it over time. It's actually easier if I show you how it works rather than try to explain to you how it works. Let's do this: we can try it on your most sensitive tooth. If it doesn't work, you don't pay. If it does work, it's only $29."*

Then, once you've applied the treatment, say this:

> *"If you start to notice sensitivity creeping back, most likely you have had more recession in that area."*

Once you have presented the case for desensitizing agents this way, you have planted a conversation in your patient's mind. If they experience sensitivity again, they probably have additional dental problems. And once you have planted that conversation, you have secured a better likelihood they will accept future treatment and case acceptance.

How Providing 5-Star Preventative Care Can Profit Your Practice

Again, look at your numbers. Here are reasonable goals to aim for:

Fluoride acceptance rate of 80%

4 sealant applications per day

4 desensitizing agent applications per day

Imagine...

If you can improve your acceptance rates for recommended preventative care (fluoride treatment, sealants, and desensitizing agents), you can reasonably expect to add...

Income from 4 sealants per day: $35,000 per year

Income from 4 desensitizing agents per day: $25,000 per year

Income from increasing your fluoride acceptance rate to 80%: $50,000

...totaling **over $100,000 per year in revenue for your practice...per hygienist!**

And your patients will be healthier, happier, and more willing to recommend your care to their friends, families, and colleagues.

Provide 5-Star Periodontal Therapy

Many dental practices are treating periodontal infection today with the same strategies and technology they used five, ten, or even many more years ago.

But times have changed. Recent research, education, and advances in technology have given us better tools, better science, and a better approach to determine the causes of periodontal infection and the most effective ways to treat and prevent it.

Dentists and hygienists can now take advantage of laser technology, oral DNA testing methods, and more effective homecare products, as well as offering additional resources like ARESTIN and other adjunct options to their patients.

Because we know so much more about the link between good oral health and its effects on overall patient systemic health, and the serious health risks posed by inflammation in the body, the practice of periodontal therapy isn't just about saving teeth anymore; it could actually be about saving lives. (We'll look at that in more detail in the next chapter.)

Providing 5-Star Periodontal Therapy all starts in the hygienist's chair.

But first, we've got to look at the numbers.

Know Your Numbers: How to Measure your Effectiveness as a Periodontal Therapist

The first thing to do is to look at your patient records over the past year and perform an audit. Of all of the patients who come in for prophylaxis, how many of them receive perio maintenance at the same time? Are you actually coding and billing separately for prophy versus perio?

It's easy to lump the two procedures together and blur the distinction between them. After all, the patient is in the chair, you're probing and recording numbers, and working the ultrasonic scaling machine in both procedures, right?

Not so fast. The cost of periodontal maintenance should be twice that of the average prophy. The hygienist must be able not only to tell the difference, they must be able to document the difference. Otherwise, you're once again leaving money on the table as well as doing your patients a disservice.

Here's one way to determine your numbers:

1. Multiply the number of patients who received a full exam during the past year by 4. That will reveal the number of possible quadrants to receive perio therapy.
2. Determine the number of actual quadrants scaled.
3. Divide the number of quadrants scaled by the total possible quadrants examined. That will give you your actual periodontal treatment percentage.

You might be surprised at the number. We've seen percentages as low as 3% and as high as 30%. What accounts for the differences?

If your percentage is very low, it's possible you haven't distinguished between perio and prophy treatments, or they are being miscoded at the billing end. It's also possible that once a patient has completed perio treatment, all of the ensuing hygiene visits are considered routine prophy visits, instead of perio maintenance.

Percentages might also be low due to a lack of financial options for the patient, or to problems in the way the treatment plan is presented.

Turning this around to provide 5-Star Periodontal Therapy requires a commitment to communicating clearly, not only among the team, but also with your patients.

How to Communicate with Patients to Deliver 5-Star Periodontal Therapy

A routine comprehensive examination is going to reveal the presence of any infection, inflammation, or bleeding that requires periodontal treatment and regular, more frequent maintenance visits. To treat the infection requires more from the patients than just a twice-a-year cleaning appointment.

Keeping the infection in check is all about the scheduling, and requires targeted, specific communication with the patient so he or she understands how critical it is.

Use your intra-oral cameras, especially the **Perio Mode** feature available on the **Sopracare,** to help patients see exactly what is going on in their mouth. As you point out the problems, follow up by outlining precisely what needs to happen.

> *"To clear up this infection we need to do three things. "*
>
> *"First, we need to do a deeper, more aggressive cleaning than you've had in the past to remove the buildup and clear the area of bacteria."*

Then pause. The patient is most likely thinking this treatment will involve pain or discomfort. Then reassure the patient by saying:

> *"We have advanced technology that enables us to be incredibly effective in dealing with bacteria without causing you pain."*

Next, tell them the second step: (Remember that people do not like to be scolded or shamed.)

> *"Second, we need to change a few things you are doing at home."*
>
> *"With this level of infection in your mouth, a power toothbrush will help you reduce or even eliminate it. We don't care where you get it, as long as you get one. We know you are busy, and we want to make everything as easy for you as possible. That's why we carry them right here in the office, and we can provide them for you at a cost less than you would pay at your local pharmacy or electronics store."*

This will help your patient understand that you are not just trying to push a sale on them; you are offering them the tools they need to be more effective against infection.

Now, talk to the patient specifically about the need for more frequent scheduling. Tie in the relationship between inflammation/infection in the mouth and overall general health.

> *"Third, to maximize healing, we need to see you back more often because the bacteria has been proven to regenerate in as few as 21-60 days after this deeper cleaning and treatment, meaning you can experience re-infection and more bleeding within that short time "*
>
> *"After we do this deep cleaning, you are starting with a clean slate. But if you don't come back every 3 months, you will end up right back where you started. If we don't stay on top of this, the disease will flare up again. It will always be there, and we MUST treat and maintain it regularly. Like any chronic condition such as diabetes, heart disease, or allergies, you will always need to maintain it."*
>
> *"Why? Because we now know that your dental health really does affect your overall health, and can be contributing to your diabetes, heart condition, (or whatever the patient might be experiencing), perhaps even making it worse."*

Presenting the solution to periodontal disease using this three-step approach will help your patient see and understand the need for treatment, especially if you have involved them in the diagnosis by showing them what's going on inside their mouth.

They might be concerned about the cost, or tell you their insurance will only pay for two hygiene appointments every year. So when presenting the perio treatment plan, offer them two options: a monthly fee for the first three months of treatment, or a total amount for the first three months of treatment, and allow them to choose.

How Providing 5-Star Periodontal Therapy Can Profit Your Practice

Once you've calculated your numbers and found your percentage of periodontal treatment rates, set goals to increase it, aiming ultimately at a 30% acceptance rate.

Track the numbers for each hygienist, and set weekly, monthly, quarterly, and yearly goals to improve them.

Make sure your staff knows the difference between prophy visits and perio visits, and then code and bill them accurately. As we said, the cost of a perio visit should be double that of a prophy visit. Careful distinctions between the two will help you recover income you might otherwise be losing. Communicate your commitment to helping your patients achieve optimal oral health. Offer them the products and tools that help them with the latest in home care.

Provide 5-Star Patient Health Advocacy

The role of every dental professional is to care for their patient's health – not just their oral health, but their overall health and wellbeing. And as the first dental professional who interacts with patients, the hygienist's role as a health advocate is critical to that care.

We can't over-stress the importance of the New Patient Interview in terms of getting to know the patient and their most important wants, needs, and values. Not only that, it will enable you to identify other health conditions that may be critically impacted by their oral health, such as diabetes, heart disease, and cancer.

The more interest you express in your patient, the more trust and rapport you will build – and that rapport is what will enable you to make recommendations and directly influence your patients to make informed decisions that contribute to their overall health

After all, it's what they expect from you. Notice how many times people ask you questions like, "Do I really need to have this done?" or, "How long can I wait before I have to get this taken care of?" They expect your opinion and recommendations.

To provide 5-Star Patient Health Advocacy, you must be committed to caring for the whole patient, using current technology, and sharing vital information in the language your patient understands. To make improvements in your service as a health advocate, you'll first need to know your numbers.

Know Your Numbers: How to Measure your Effectiveness as a Patient Health Care Advocate

The first place to look to determine your effectiveness as a Patient Health Care Advocate is your Treatment Acceptance rate.

It should be a simple matter to calculate the number of new patients you see, the number of Treatment Plans you present (and the dollars they represent), and the number of Treatment Plans your patients accept.

If you're unhappy with your numbers, you'll need to make some changes.

What tools do you use to present the case? Do you use them consistently? Do you involve your patients in their own diagnoses? Is the entire team, from the front desk to the hygienist to the dentist to the billing department involved in treatment planning and presentation? Is the entire team committed to linking oral health with the patient's overall health? Are you all "on the same page" in terms of communicating with your patients?

The national average for treatment acceptance rates is 61%. If you are not achieving rates of 90% or better, you are leaving money on the table.

How to Communicate with Patients to Deliver 5-Star Patient Health Advocacy

Assess your own practice. Do you actively emphasize the benefits of treating the whole patient with comprehensive care? Or are you focusing only on treating your patient "one tooth at a time?" Do you and your team use scripts and all available technological help to keep the presentations on target and guide your patients to "yes?"

Let's start here. How many times have you heard questions like these when proposing a comprehensive treatment plan to your patients?

> *"I need to check with my spouse."*
>
> *"Let me check my work schedule and get back with you."*
>
> *"I will schedule when we get back from vacation in 2 months."*

Patients who don't accept treatment and use objections like these are most likely driven by one (or more) of three primary emotions:

1. **Confusion**
   We may be using terminology the patient simply doesn't understand. We're speaking "dental-ese" instead of using plain, ordinary terms.
2. **Overwhelm**
   We may be presenting too much information all at once, not communicating in a way that guarantees the patient understands each step before we move on to presenting the next.
3. **Frustration**
   They may have upcoming plans they fear will have to be put on hold in order to undergo treatment, or they may worry about expenses that they hadn't planned for.

The hygienist's job (and really, the job of the entire team), is to recognize these emotions when we encounter them and actively communicate with our patients to guide them through them.

1. **To eliminate confusion**, speak in terms your patients will understand. Better yet, use your available technology to **show them while you tell them**.
   For example, you can use the cavity-detecting laser (Diagnodent) to help patients see for themselves what you are describing. Have patients hold it, so they are participating in their own diagnosis. They will hear the alarm signals, see the numbers as you work, and recognize there are problems.

   > *"Let me have you hold this machine while I show you the problem that concerns me. You'll hear a series of beeps, and see a number on the screen that indicates the degree of the damage."*

   Follow up using the intra-oral camera, and show them what the problem looks like on a large screen.

   > *"As you can see on the screen, that crack in your tooth is serious. No wonder it hurts when you eat! If we don't get it taken care of, you're at greater risk of increasing pain, not to mention infection which can seriously compromise your cardio-vascular disease and put your health at risk."*

   Using just these two technologies, your patients will see the problem and feel a greater sense of urgency as you describe the consequences to their health of leaving it untreated and express your concern.

2. **To reduce overwhelm, show the patient one problem at a time**, (using the techniques above) and make sure they understand it before you move on to the next. Instead of asking, "Do you understand?", ask instead:

   > *"I know I've given you a lot of information to process. What questions or concerns do you have about what we've discovered?"*

3. **To reduce frustration, make sure you emphasize value** – what the patient values in particular. Your patients will find a way to pay for what they really want, so your job is to focus on helping them **want** to have their teeth taken care of to avoid future pain and prevent possible health complications (consequences), and a greater sense of satisfaction with their smile (value).

4. That means you need to distinguish between consequences (pain) and value (pleasure), and focus on the direct benefits rather than the technicalities of the procedure. For example:

> *"If this was my mouth, I wouldn't hesitate to go ahead with implants. Let me tell you why."*
>
> *"When we put the implants in your mouth, they will feel almost like natural teeth. It will feel great to finally be able to chew without pain, you won't have to take anything out to clean, and you will be able to brush and floss these teeth just like you did before. Not only that, but the implants will have porcelain crowns that will look incredibly like your own natural teeth."*

Or...

> *"I know it seems overwhelming, maybe even a bit frustrating, since you were hoping this would be just a 'quick fix' and then you'd be on your way. But the benefit of getting those cracked teeth replaced with implants now is going to impact your health directly, especially given the link we now know exists between dental problems and diabetes."* (Or heart disease, or obesity, or cancer, or other health problem the patient may be experiencing.)

If you approach your hygiene department as if you were a the owner of a total health-care business owner, if you build value by keeping things simple, and if you use scripted questions, carefully crafted responses, and intelligently designed treatment plans, you will begin to see improvements. Your production numbers will increase, your treatment acceptance rates will rise, and your patients' health will improve.

How Providing 5-Star Patient Advocacy Can Profit Your Practice

Here are some numbers to consider:

1. 65% of all production completed in restorative is referred by hygiene.

2. 80% of revenue from a patient comes within in their first 18 months with your practice.

That means that the hygienist is a critical player in driving patient care – and resulting revenue -- in any dental practice.

When you look critically at your examination procedures, listen critically to yourself as you communicate your findings with your patients, and make changes to the way you present your recommendations, you can dramatically improve the contribution the hygienist role makes to the practice.

Audit your case acceptance rate. If you find it's less than 90%, analyze where to make changes. Change the way you communicate with your patients. Stress simplicity, value, and health benefits. Use the available technology as teaching aids, as you educate your patients and show them the value of treatment. Develop scripts for every procedure: from your greeting, to the questions you ask, to the responses you give, to the examination itself, and to the presentation of the treatment plan.

When you are consistent with your commitment to providing valuable health care, your practice's bottom line will show it.

Develop a 5-Star Dentist/Hygienist Partnership

The key to developing a 5-Star Partnership between the hygienist and the dentist is **effective, focused, consistent communication**, both behind the scenes and in front of patients.

When the dentist and the hygienist work together to **develop communication systems** for everything – the new patient interview, the initial exam, follow-up exams, prophylaxes, perio treatments, treatment plan presentations – and when they use those systems consistently, practice revenues rise dramatically, patient satisfaction improves, and the workplace hums with purpose.

Many practices that experience frustration, low morale, high inter-employee drama, and low production numbers can trace their dysfunction and low profit to a systems failure. Picture a Viking ship with a dozen people at the oars. They're aiming at an island, the wind is howling, the seas are rough. And yet each one is rowing by himself, at his own pace, following his own idea of how to get to the island. Imagine the chaos with a dozen rowers' oars crashing into one another, each following its own pace and rhythm. Imagine the arguing. Imagine the inefficiency. Imagine how long it's going to take them to get anywhere! It's a systems failure.

You can transform your practice by conducting a careful audit of the communication systems you have in place (or don't have in place). That will allow you to see the systems that work, and design fixes for the systems that don't. Once the entire team understands the new system and each team member follows careful scripts for interacting with patients and with one another -- scripts focused on providing 5-Star Patient Care -- they are all working toward the same goal, in effect, rowing in the same direction.

In this chapter, we'll focus on three specific communication systems that will make the biggest difference in the way the hygienist/dentist partnership works: perfecting patient handoffs, increasing treatment plan acceptance rates, and communicating in front of patients for maximum impact.

Provide 5-Star Patient Handoffs

Your patients, like customers of any business, want to know they are valued. They expect service, care, and concern for their wellbeing. They want to feel heard. When they do not feel valued, important, or heard, when they feel they are just a backside with teeth in a treatment chair, or when they feel pressured to buy something they don't think they need, they will flee your practice. You'll never see them again. And they will probably never tell you why.

The way the hygienist hands off the patient to the dentist is critical to making the patient feel valued, important, and special. It's also the key to "selling" without effort, pressure, or manipulation. Once you perfect the patient handoff, you will find your revenues growing as patients more willingly accept your recommended treatment plans.

1. The foundation for the perfect handoff is how much you know about what your patients want, need, and value. You build that foundation by asking the right questions, and listening to your patient's answers.
   Your New Patient Interview, Smile Sheet, or questionnaire will give you basic information. As you perform the initial exam, you'll want to ask questions that will help you understand what your patient wants, needs, and values. Consider questions like these:

   > *"I am going to take some photos of your teeth, to show you and the doctor things you cannot see with the naked eye. It's important for us to get to know our patients as people before we get to know your teeth, so I'd like to ask you a few questions as I take the photos. Is that okay with you?"*

   > *"Although you're a new patient for us, it's pretty obvious you've been to other dentists before. What treatments have you had, other than having your teeth cleaned?"*
   >
   > *"Tell me about your last dentist. Is there anything you really liked about him or her? If there is, we'll do our best to make sure we do the same things for you."*
   >
   > *"Likewise, is there anything you didn't like about your last dentist? If there is, we'll do our best to make sure you don't experience that here."*

"What do you know about the dental health of your family – parents, grandparents? We know that like general health, your dental health can be shaped by your genetics."

"You indicate you're pretty healthy. But speaking of your family health, is there any history of cancer, diabetes, heart disease, or stroke? I ask because we know that your oral health has a direct link with your overall, general health."

"On a scale of 1-10, where 10 is perfect, how would you rate the health and appearance of your teeth?"

"What would have to change for you to give yourself a 10?"

"Do you have any other special concerns? Any events coming up like graduations, anniversaries, or vacations?"

"Tell me a little about your job. Do you deal face-to-face with customers? Do you have to go out and meet the public? Are you confident you look your best?"

Questions like these help you get to know your patient as a person, understand what's important to that person, and prepare you to hand off efficiently to the doctor. If you use Diagnodent in your practice, adapt its Screening Form to your needs.

As you ask questions, listen carefully to what the patient tells you. Let their answers guide your conversation. Make notes about the answers in the patient's file, so the doctor will have that information and refer to it in his or her treatment.

Be sure to include questions about any dental work you find: crowns, silver fillings, root canals, or failing prostheses.

"How do you feel about that old silver crown?" "Are you happy with the discoloration of that one veneer?" "How long have you had those silver fillings?"

2. During the exam, include the patient in his or her own diagnosis. Have the patient hold the Diagnodent laser, use the intra-oral camera, and make sure the patient can see, hear, and understand what you are looking at. As you proceed through the exam, make notes about mandatory, elective, or cosmetic treatments you will be recommending.
   And for goodness sakes, speak common, everyday words your patients will understand – avoid jargon, abbreviations, and acronyms that represent "dentist-ese."

3. When the doctor comes in, have your summary ready to go so you can share it in two or three minutes. A smooth handoff will be conducted in front of the patient, using the patient's own words as much as possible, and it will include:
   - An introduction, if the patient is new, including any information about how they heard about the practice or who referred them.
   - The reason for the patient visit.
   - Asking the patient for permission to share what you learned with the doctor.
   - A summary of the patient's answers to your questions as you conducted the exam.
   - A summary of the exam or treatments you performed, including any problems you discovered.
   - A summary of the treatment options you and the patient discussed, broken down into mandatory, elective, and cosmetic options.

Here's what a typical new patient handoff might sound like:

> *"Doctor, this is Jim Smith. He works with Charlotte Roberts, and she recommends us to Jim. He came in today for a routine cleaning and exam."*
>
> *"Jim, I'd like to share with doctor what we talked about, is that okay with you?"*
>
> *"Doctor, Jim expressed concern about the old silver fillings in his back molars, and wondered about what options there might be to replace them. He's also concerned about some pain he experiences while eating, particularly around those old silver fillings."*
>
> *"I told him about the research that indicates we should replace the old silver/mercury amalgams with new fillings, and he agreed that he considers replacing them a mandatory treatment, for health reasons."*
>
> *"We also talked about the options for veneers to help close the gap in his front upper teeth, and although he sees the possibilities, he considers getting them to be a cosmetic procedure and is concerned his insurance won't cover it."*
>
> *"Jim is excited, because his son is graduating college next month, and he needs to travel out of state to attend. He's wondering if we can get the most important work scheduled to be complete so it doesn't interrupt his plans."*

Summarizing your conversation, the treatment, and the exam, in front of the patient, **using the patient's own words**, illustrates that you were listening, that you heard them, and that you care about their concerns. It makes the patient feel valued, important, and cared for.

Summarizing in front of the patient also sets the doctor up to win with the patient, provides the most important needs for the doctor to focus on, and saves valuable time because the doctor won't have to gather all of this information from scratch.

Work Together to Develop 5-Star Treatment Acceptance Rates

The traditional model of running a dental practice is basically authoritarian. The dentist, the highly educated professional, held the power over the patient. He or she told patients what to do, when to do it, and how to do it, never mind the cost. Patients occupied a more passive role, accepting (or resisting) the dentist's advice and professional opinion. In that old model, any dentist who wanted to grow his or her practice had to become more aggressive at "selling" the patient on treatment the dentist deemed necessary. It was an aggressive model, and it has become woefully outdated.

Why? It doesn't work anymore.

You see, today's dental patients know they have choices about where to get treatment. They know that if their dentist doesn't meet their needs and address their values, they can always find another dentist in the community who will work better for them. They demand something that used to be unheard of in the medical profession: customer service. And because patients have changed, the model of successful dentistry has had to change to survive.

What does that have to do with treatment acceptance rates?

Plenty.

The hygienist and the dentist, in partnership, need to act as service-oriented **consultants** to their patients, and they are going to have to develop more effective persuasion skills.

Patients do not want to be sold, told, shamed, or ordered into treatment. They want to be advised and consulted, taking their values, needs, and desires into account. They want options. They want to explore possibilities. They want to be treated like human beings.

That is why it is so critical to invest time in getting to know your patients by asking the kinds of questions that dig deep, letting their answers guide your responses. The kinds of questions you ask will help you learn what your patients value, what they want, and what they need to get what they want.

During your exam or treatment, don't just ask simple "yes or no" questions. Ask the kinds of questions that get you a bit of a story or explanation, like these:

> *"How do you feel about that discoloration at your gum line?"*
>
> *"Are you having any sensitivity to heat or cold on any of these teeth?"*
>
> *"Are you more concerned with just getting by, or would you like more information about this kind of thing in the future?"*
>
> *"Would you be interested to know there are alternatives to silver fillings? Let me share the current thinking about those and tell you about options for replacing them."*
>
> *"That looks like an old temporary crown. How long have you had it?"*
>
> *"Are you interested in a solution that will work for the long-term?"*
>
> *"As you get older, how much dentistry do you want to have to plan for?"*
>
> *Do you like the space between your front teeth? If we could show you a way to close it, would you be interested?"*

The answers to these questions, along with getting your patient's agreement about what treatment is mandatory, what treatment is elective, and what treatment is cosmetic, will help you design the optimum treatment plan.

When presenting the plan to your patients, give them options: Mandatory, Elective, and Cosmetic options, based on your understanding of their wants, needs, and values. Show them the benefits of each, and explain the consequences of not getting treatment. And make sure you explain payment options clearly, showing them the value of investing in their values rather than just "buying treatment."

Demonstrate 5-Star Communication in Front of Patients

Do you remember what you used to call *caries*? Or what you used to call *alloy restorations*? How about *inflammatory degenerative disease*? Or this one: *maxillary right third molar*? Well, your patients call them cavities, silver fillings, infection, and wisdom tooth.

So imagine your patient, sitting in the chair during the handoff, and you say to the dentist, *"Mr. Jenkins here has deteriorating alloy restorations on numbers 28, and 30 with marginal caries. He is going to need full amalgam restorations on those. He's also experiencing pain in the maxillary right third molar, which may require extraction."*

How is your patient going to hear this? Is he even going to understand you? You might as well be speaking some alien language.

How about this example? During your exam, you find Mr. Jenkins has some *"anterior tooth attrition, inadequate anterior guidance, and age/stress-related cervical abfractions."*

How is he going to react, hearing you say this over the top of him?

If you have asked Mr. Jenkins about his wants, needs, and values, he might have told you, in his own words, that he's concerned that his front teeth are discolored and he's embarrassed at dealing face-to-face with his customers.

Wouldn't it make more sense to speak about him, in front of him, using the language he speaks and understands? Wouldn't it make more sense to speak over him in a way that addresses his values, wants, and needs?

> *"Mr. Jenkins, I can understand why you are concerned about dealing face-to-face with your customers, because your front teeth are worn and discolored. That's a simple fix. We can polish away the discolored enamel and replace it with a very durable material. It'll take only two visits, just three weeks apart."*

The key to demonstrating 5-Star communication in front of patients is to respect them by speaking in terms they understand.

In some industries, there's a clear distinction between "front of the house" and "back of the house." "Front of the house" refers to any interactions that patients can see and hear. "Back of the house" refers, then, to those interactions that should be invisible to the patient.

The Golden Rule is to keep "front of the house" interactions between the dentist and hygienist calm, courteous, and respectful of the patient; and save arguments, conflicts, corrections or complaints for the "back of the house" where they belong.

The way the dentist and hygienist interact with each other should demonstrate respect for the patient in the chair in front of them. Simple courtesy, please and thank you, and a calm, reassuring tone of voice go a long way in putting patients at ease.

Developing a 5-Star dentist/hygienist partnership demands paying special attention to the communication systems you have in place in your practice. If your partnership is not where you'd like it to be, conduct a "systems audit," examine your communication systems, and work together to deliver consistent, effective communication with one another and most especially with your patients. Your practice will grow and thrive if you do!

Produce 5-Star Hygiene Profitability

How much does your Hygiene department contribute to your practice? What is your productivity rate per hour, as a hygienist? What goal should you set for hourly or daily productivity? What does downtime in your hygiene department cost the practice?

If you don't know your numbers, how do you know if your hygienist is profitable?

How do you measure up?

Know and track hygiene numbers

If you haven't already done it, you need to perform a productivity audit, by hygienist and other care provider in your practice. Go through your patient billing for the past year, and see how you stack up to the following national averages and benchmarks:

Here are some national averages and benchmarks to consider:

- The national average daily productivity for a hygienist is $61.00 (2009 figures)
- A healthy, profitable hygiene department produces 25-35% of gross practice revenue
- Hygiene discovers up to 75% of restorative needs in patient visits, and is in the best position to recommend both restorative and elective procedures
- Periodontics accounts for 1/3 of all hygiene codes billed
- In a healthy practice, the hygiene department should only experience between 5-8% downtime
- A productive hygienist should produce revenue equal to about three times their wages

It may seem like a daunting task, and if you fear it will take too much of your time, get your accountant/bookkeeper to help.

How to Keep the Hygiene Schedule Full: Recall, Recovery, and Reactivation

Given the overhead in the average dental practice, it's to everybody's benefit to keep the schedule full. If you don't focus on the schedule every day, you will end up in a "feast or famine" situation, with some days a crowded schedule, and other days a vacant one.

Everybody in the practice should be focused on this effort – the front desk, the hygienist, the practice manager/office manager, and the back office – and you should have a system in place, with a designated person in charge, whenever you have slack in your schedule. After all, **when the hygiene schedule is full, so is the dentist's**. And when both are full, the practice grows and becomes more profitable for everyone.

Design procedures for **re-calling** your patients who are due for a hygiene visit, **recovering** time when you have cancellations, missed appointments, or holes in the schedule, and **reactivating** those patients you haven't seen in a while who are overdue for their appointments. Let's examine these systems in some detail:

Recall

How many of your patients leave without scheduling their next hygiene appointment? If it's not close to 100%, you're going to end up with patient attrition and holes in the schedule six months from now. Make it a goal that "nobody gets out of here without an appointment." As patients leave, part of the checkout procedure should be setting their next appointment.

Your system should also include reminders/confirmations. Plan your first reminder one week prior to the patient's scheduled appointment, asking them to call or email you to confirm. If you find people who want to reschedule, you'll at least have a week to fill the hole in the schedule. Let them know in this call or email that you will be phoning them the day before their appointment as a courtesy.

If you don't receive a confirmation by 48 hours before the scheduled appointment, call the patient to remind them of their appointment. Do not offer them the chance to cancel or reschedule. **Do not ask them to confirm, tell them you are expecting them!**

If you find you have patients who have not scheduled an appointment for six months after a visit, you should be able to track them in your system. Call them anyway, and simply tell them *"I'm calling you about your dental appointment next week."* They will say, "Wait a minute, I don't have an appointment next week," to which you can reply (with a smile), *"I know, that's why I'm calling – to help you schedule one!"*

Recovery

When you find you have open times in your schedule, whether from cancellations or just because it's a light day, you can work smart to fill the schedule. Again, everyone in the practice should be focused on this, so it's not a last-minute scramble to fill the schedule.

First, create an "ASAP" list. As patients leave, while they make appointments, ask them "*If we end up having an earlier opening in our schedule, would you like us to let you know?*" This list should be no longer than 50-75 patients, and should NOT contain patients who habitually forget or cancel their appointments. When you call people on your ASAP list, they will feel special when you say, "*You asked us to let you know if we had an earlier opening in our schedule. We have a last-minute change in the schedule for Tuessday, and you were the first person we thought of.*"

You can also look ahead to next week's schedule, to see if any of next week's patients can come in earlier than planned. Many of them will agree.

And third, you can look at today's schedule for opportunities that patients you are seeing today for other treatment can be flexible enough for a routine cleaning or perio maintenance treatment.

Reactivation

Reactivation is mounting a campaign to get those patients who you haven't seen in 18 months or more to come in and resume treatment. There may be many reasons you don't see these patients: they might no longer be living in the area; they might be comfortable thinking there's no reason to come in because nothing is bothering them; or they might simply have found another dentist.

Many practices give up on these patients, but they can be a hidden source of revenue.

It's going to take more than a phone call or an email to get them back in. That's why you should consider it a campaign and not just stop after leaving a few voice mail messages. Your campaign should be creative, and could include things like:

- A letter
- A phone call
- A postcard
- A second phone call
- An interesting mail piece (odd-sized colored envelope, a "lumpy" piece like a toothbrush, or other attention-grabbing device) that is irresistible for the patient to open.

Speak to the patient directly, focused on concern for their wellbeing. *"We've missed you!"* or *"We haven't seen you in a while, and we hope you are okay!"* express that sentiment effectively.

It might take some time and creative thinking, but design your campaign and then go through your patient records to find and "reactivate" those lost patients and recover the revenue they represent to your practice.

Set and Re-evaluate Goals

Perform a productivity audit for your practice, and get everyone in hygiene accustomed to tracking his or her own productivity.

To give you some context, here are some benchmarks for each hygienist to aim at:

Metric	**Target**
Fluoride	80% acceptance rate
Sealant	4 treatments/day
De-sensitizing agents	4 treatments/day
Prophylaxis	6-8 patients/day
Periodontal maintenance	2-3 patients/day
Treatment Acceptance Rates	90% or better

Once you've found your actual productivity numbers, begin to set goals to raise those numbers week by week. Here are some ways to help you improve them:

1. As we discussed in Chapter 1, fluoride, sealants, and de-sensitizing agents alone can contribute up to $100,000 per year to your practice, if you are comfortable taking control of the conversation and confident in recommending treatment to your patients. Write yourself scripts – use and review index cards if you need to – and practice effective language until you are comfortable and the language is your own.

2. Since hygiene accounts for 75% of recommended restoration work, get comfortable speaking to the patient about what you discover during exams and treatment, and make sure your handoffs are smooth, and the language you use in front of your patients is clear and focused on the benefits of treatment.

3. Take a good hard look at how you are coding hygienist treatments, to make sure you are making a distinction between regular prophys and periodontal maintenance, and you are coding and billing appropriately. As we mentioned in Chapter 1, perio maintenance should be billed at about twice what you are billing for prophys.

4. To improve your treatment acceptance rates, use all available technology, in partnership with the dentist, to "show and tell" your patients about the conditions you find during treatment and exams. Stress benefits (both short-term and long-term) to getting treatment now versus later, focused on what the patient tells you about their values, needs, and wants. Make sure you have resources available to offer your patients regarding financing, insurance, and monthly payment options to show your patients that investing in their oral health doesn't have to be a financial burden.

5. And perhaps most important of all, keep the hygiene schedule full, to eliminate costly downtime, aiming at no more than 8% hygiene downtime. Use any downtime to keep the schedule full!

Hygiene Protocol with Patients

1. Explain to Every patient what probing numbers mean
2. Ask patient to listen and count all numbers over 3
3. Verbalize All probing depths to patient
4. Explain how many bleeding points/percentage to patients
5. Print out perio chart
6. In red, mark All bleeding points
7. Highlight All depths above 3, count them and circle the total amount
8. Show & review the perio chart with patient and give to treatment coordinator to review with patient and place in treatment plan folder

Comparison Chart – Periodontal Maintenance vs. Prophylaxis

What are the differences between prophylaxis and periodontal maintenance?

Periodontal Maintenance

- Therapeutic
- Following surgical or non-surgical gum therapy
- Removal of toxins from root surfaces
- To disinfect and control disease progression
- Remove plaque, bacteria, and calculus below the gum line to control disease
- Needed every 3-4 months
- Gum disease is episodic in nature and can be triggered by stress, disease and other systemic problems
- Gum disease is not curable but is controllable
- To maintain the health and function of the gums, bone and supporting structures

Prophylaxis

- Preventative
- Lacking signs of disease
- Healthy tissue
- No pockets greater than 4 mm
- No bleeding upon probing
- Remove plaque and stain above the gum line
- Non-therapeutic treatment
- Needed every at least every 6 months

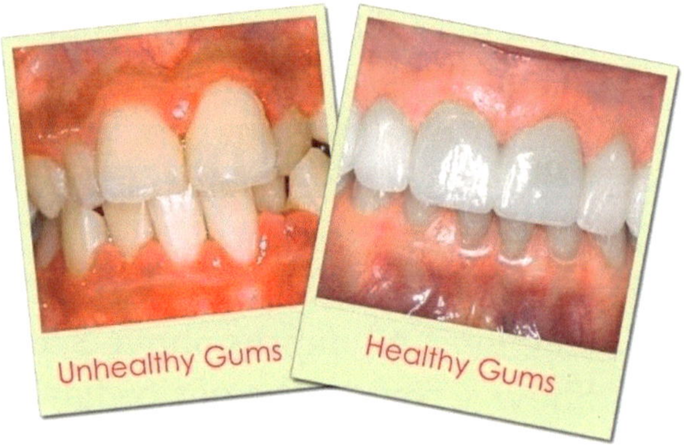

**Your dental hygienist is an important part of your healthcare team. Our dental hygienists are experts at what they do and will recommend and provide you the best treatment that is customized to you.*

Hygiene Visit Checklist - Patient Name: ______________________

Procedures	**Check ✓**
Greeting patient in reception area with handshake	
Office tour (new patients only)	
Seating patient	
Offer Amenities	
Update & review medical history	
Review Smile Questionnaire and/or Emotional Motivator	
Inquire about any dental concerns	
Take blood pressure	
Oral cancer screening	
Periodontal assessment and perio charting (use script)	
Caries risk assessment	
Malocclusion Assessment	
Head and neck exam	
Capture photos on intra oral camera	
Capturing digital radiographs	
Discuss with patients your concerns and findings using Emotional Motivator	
Introduce patient to doctor, then doctor to patient.	
Give patient router to doctor.	
***Hand-Off** (Discuss observations and dental needs with patient & again with Doctor)	
Enter treatment plan following doctor exam	
Scaling	
Polishing	
Fluoride	
Plaque control and dispensing of oral hygiene instruction & aids	
Schedule continuing care and periodontal appointments	
Confirm today's treatment in the computer and set appt complete	
***Hand-Off** to tx coordinator or check out	
Give patient router to tx coordinator	
Decontaminate treatment rooms	
Sterilize instruments	
Set up treatment room for next patient	

Hand-Off Checklist to Doctor	**Check ✓**
Problems (Concerns)	
Consequences of these problems/concerns	
Emotional Motivator (i.e. Wants to not ever have dentures.)	
Solution (What you want to do? Recommend?)	

Hand-Off Checklist to Tx Coordinator	**Check ✓**
What was done today?	
What tx recommended?	
What clinical reasons for the tx recommended? (Problems)	
What are the consequences of not doing the treatment? (Consequences)	
State the patient's emotional motivator.	
State if the appointment has been scheduled.	
*Give router to tx coordinator.	

Hygiene Cancellation Protocol

- Cancellations will be alternated between Hygienists, taking turns with the missing appt.
- Cancellations will also be handled by assessing the big picture of the Practice's needs first (what makes the most sense in terms of the existing schedule as relates to the patients' needs)
- The following checklist IS in order of Priority and notes to demonstrate what has been done will account for productive time spent (keeps the team informed)

DATE		NOTES
	Call Canceled & No-Show Patients – Create Urgency	
	Optimize Hygiene Schedule 2 days out	
	Routers Highlighted/Ready For Next Day	
	Call Unconfirmed Patients 24-48 Hours	
	Sharpen Hygiene Instruments	
	Check on Stocked Products (ordering up to date?)	
	Stock Hygiene Room	
	Clean, assist with Sterilization	
	Maintenance on Hygiene Equipment	

12 Facts You Can't Ignore

About the Mouth-Body Connection

1. 80% of American adults over 35 have some form of gum disease.
2. 95% of Americans who have diabetes also have periodontal disease.
3. Nearly HALF of Americans have periodontitis, the most severe form of periodontal disease.
4. Oral bacteria have been implicated in the development of Alzheimer's disease and dementia.
5. Over 25 million Americans suffer from obstructive sleep apnea, a condition associated with diabetes, heart disease, high blood pressure, obesity, and car accidents.
6. Periodontal treatment helps people with diabetes control their blood sugar better.
7. Treating gum disease lowers annual medical costs associated with diabetes, stroke, heart disease, and pregnancy.
8. People with gum disease are nearly twice as likely to suffer from heart disease.
9. Bacteria in the mouth have been linked to oral, esophageal, lung, colorectal, pancreatic, and breast cancers.
10. Oral bacteria travel through the bloodstream and can have an effect on many organs and processes.
11. Gum disease can interfere with the success of knee replacement surgery.
12. Women with severe periodontal disease were found to have seven times the risk of giving birth early as women who had healthy gums. They also had seven times the risk of having a baby with a low birth weight. Oral bacteria traveling through the bloodstream have been found to cause stillbirth.

Source: The American Association for Oral Systemic Health

Are You at Risk for Future Health Problems?

Directions: Complete the risk assessment checklist below and talk to your healthcare provider about how you might be able to lower your risk.

Heart Disease	Alzheimer's
☐ Family history of heart disease ☐ Uncontrolled hypertension (high blood pressure) ☐ Abnormal cholesterol levels ☐ High stress levels ☐ Smoking status ☐ Obesity ☐ Sedentary Lifestyle ☐ Bleeding and/or inflamed gums	☐ Age 65 or older ☐ Family history of Alzheimer's ☐ History of head trauma ☐ Heart disease/stroke ☐ Insulin resistance and diabetes
Diabetes	**Airway Occlusion**
☐ Family history of diabetes ☐ Bleeding gums ☐ Sedentary lifestyle ☐ Insulin resistance ☐ Overweight/Obese ☐ Had gestational diabetes ☐ High blood pressure ☐ Abnormal cholesterol levels	☐ Snoring ☐ Mouth breathing ☐ Obesity ☐ Daytime sleepiness ☐ Large/thick neck ☐ Falling asleep while sitting, watching TV, or driving ☐ Headaches ☐ Jaw pain and/or limited movement in the jaw ☐ Worn, broken, or cracked teeth ☐ Clicking or popping sounds in the jaw ☐ Persistent shoulder and/or neck pain ☐ Uncomfortable bite ☐ Chronic congestion in the nose and/or ears

Source: The American Association of Oral Systemic Health

Do You Have Periodontal Disease?

Read the following symptoms, and check any that you are experiencing:

- ☐ My gums bleed.
- ☐ My gums are red or swollen.
- ☐ My gums are loose, and seem to move away from my teeth.
- ☐ My gums seem to have receded from areas in my mouth, making some of my teeth appear longer.
- ☐ I have a bad taste in my mouth.
- ☐ Some of my teeth feel loose.
- ☐ I have lots of fillings, bridges, or crowns in my mouth.
- ☐ I currently suffer from diabetes, heart disease, rheumatoid arthritis, osteopenia, or an unusual amount of stress.
- ☐ I do not brush and floss at least twice a day?

If you checked any of the above statements, you stand a good chance of suffering from some form of periodontal disease (gum disease), and you need treatment to minimize and manage the symptoms.

Unfortunately, once your Dental Professional has diagnosed you with periodontal disease, you will always have it. It cannot be cured. But frequent, thorough periodontal cleanings and proper home care will help you keep it under control.

You can, however, prevent periodontal disease as long as none of the other risk factors are present. With proper home care and consistent visits to your dentist or periodontist, you can improve your chances of avoiding gum disease in the first place.

Other Risk Factors for Periodontal Disease

Smoking or Tobacco Use

Recent studies indicate that using tobacco might be THE most significant risk factor for developing periodontal or gum disease.

Genetics

Despite your oral health regimen, you might be more susceptible to gum disease simply because of your genetics. Your Oral Systemic Dentist or Periodontist can administer simple genetic tests to help determine if your genetics put you at risk for developing periodontal disease in your lifetime, and what you can do to treat it.

Stress

Many diseases are linked to stress, including periodontal disease. When you are experiencing stress, your body cannot fight infections effectively, and therefore your risk for developing inflammatory diseases (including periodontal disease) increases.

Medication

Some oral contraceptives, anti-depressants, heart medications, and certain other drugs, can effect your oral health. Keep your periodontist and primary care dentist informed of all medications you are currently taking. Some modern drugs including Statins can deplete your body of certain essential vitamins and minerals. Your Oral Systemic practice can also help you evaluate your needs.

Systemic Diseases

If you suffer from inflammatory diseases including heart disease, high blood pressure, or diabetes, you are at a higher risk for developing gum disease. When systemic diseases like these are not controlled, they can contribute to the development of periodontal disease because they make it harder for your body to naturally fight inflammation and infection.

Restorative Dental Work

Any dental work has a limited life span. Fillings, crowns, or bridges can leak or break over time. If you have experienced a lot of restorative dental work, you might be at greater risk for periodontal disease. It can be difficult to clean around restorative work, leading to hidden spaces that can more easily harbor bacteria. Without proper home care and regular dental visits, you are unknowingly helping these bacteria multiply and cause periodontal disease.

What Happens in Your Mouth...Does Not Stay in Your Mouth

The Oral-Systemic Facts

Your mouth talks to your body...

- At least 80% of American adults have gum inflammation/ disease.
- Gum disease is linked with blood vessel disease, heart attacks and strokes.
- Gum disease and tooth loss increases risk of Alzheimer's disease.
- If you have diabetes and bleeding gums, your risk of premature death increases by 400 to 700 percent.
- Gum disease increases risk for head & neck cancer, and pancreatic and kidney cancer.

...and your body talks to your mouth!

- Increased trigeminal nerve traffic from TMJ and bad dental bite can create central sensitization and migraines.
- Poor ventilation during sleep triggers nighttime clenching and bracing to maintain the airway.
- Bad bites and poor oral-facial development increases risk for sleep apnea.
- Cavities are caused by acid-loving bacteria spread during kissing and sharing food.
- Oral bacteria are being found in brain tissue, heart vessels, joints, and many other parts of your body.

Source: The American Academy for Oral Systemic Health

Diode Laser

Benefits:

- Extreme patient comfort compared to other options
- Produces less trauma so typically less anesthesia is needed
- Decrease in post-op discomfort following scaling & root planning
- Faster so less time in the chair
- Minimized anxiety
- Reduces swelling
- Better bleeding indices
- Improved tissue color and contour
- Reattachment occurring at a faster rate than traditional SRP with no laser integration
- Road to recovery quicker
- Increases precision
- Cost Effective For Patient: Decrease overall cost than using antibiotic therapy (Arestin, Atridox, Periochip)

We are excited about our Diode laser because we want to provide you the highest level of service possible and our laser increases your comfort by allowing us to do more with less anesthesia which is beneficial to your body and your health.

Enhanced Oral Cancer Screening - Oral ID $20-$35

SHOCKING FACTS ABOUT ORAL CANCER:

- Oral cancer causes 1 American death every hour
- The incidence of oral cancer and throat cancer in the United States is 34,000 new cases per year, with only 57% living more than 5 years and an average of 8,000 deaths per year.
- Oral cancer can be painful and disfiguring, and can destroy the ability to taste and enjoy food.
- Oral cancer has one of the highest death rates of any cancer since it is often caught only after is has metastasized to the lymph nodes.
- More than 25% of oral cancer victims Do Not Use tobacco, Alcohol or have other lifestyle risks

THE KEY TO SURVIVAL IS EARLY DIAGNOSIS WHICH INCREASES THE CURE RATE TO GREATER THAN 80%

- We have invested in this technology because it potentially can save your life.

The Difference Between an Exam and a Screening

1.____.

2. . _______________________________________.

3. . _______________________________________.

Now we have a new technology call Oral-ID. This allows us to see early changes in your oral tissues under a special hand-held light. We are incorporating the use of the Oral-ID Cancer Screening into our standard oral exam by our hygienists because it gives us a new level of detection.

Questions to Discuss Occlusal Guards

Have you ever had a time when you woke up not feeling rested?

Have you ever experienced jaw or joint pain?

Has your jaw ever felt tired in the morning?

Do you wake or experience headaches during the day?

Oftentimes, your teeth may start loosening and you will feel pain in your gums because of clenching your teeth too much.

A custom fit occlusal guard does not treat the problems, but is a preventative measure against more serious problems caused by long-term teeth grinding.

If your symptoms are left unchecked and continue too long without being taken care of, more dental problems, such a fractured teeth and tooth loss, will likely occur and will be much more costly in the long run.

Patient Five Star Service

Patient Comfort Menu

To Create A Pleasant Experience For You

PATIENT COMFORT MENU

BEVERAGE CENTER

Complimentary Coffee, Tea and Water available at all times to you during your visit

PILLOW

Relax your neck and shoulders with our soft pillows

THE COZY BLANKET

Enjoy our soothing and comfortable blanket wrapped around you

NITRIOUS OXIDE

Laughing gas or conscious sedation can be administered to reduce your anxiety and make the time pass quickly

COMPLIMENTARY WiFi

Type your WiFi address and Login HERE

Your LOGO Goes HERE

New Patient Call Protocol

Name?			
Reason for calling?		**Pain/Symptoms?**	
Agree on an Appointment time…			
How did you hear about our office? Get Details			
Medications?			
Drug Allergies?			
Dental Insurance?			
How long since last dental visit?			
Other appointments for family members?			
Cell Phone/Email			

Things to remember on a call:

- SMILES so the patient can HEAR your smile
- INTRODUCE yourself
- LISTEN to the Person as more than a patient, listen to their story and decode their primary language (Visual, Kinesthetic, Auditory, Digital Auditory)
- USE the patients name while speaking to them, USE the patient's own words and tone
- Repeat the patient's appointment time and any details important to the call
- THANK the patient for the call
- WRITE with INITITALS and DATELINE detailed information about the reason for the call, make it long as needs be, remember, you are explaining the purpose to people who will need to know without you being there to explain.

P/C/EM/S

Problem

Consequences

Emotional **M**otivator – Time, Pain, Money

Solution

Example:

"I want you to get on my schedule this week because (lists 3 consequences of not taking action now) and those are going to be more painful (kinesthetic), cost you more money (Logical) and require more appointments (Time)."

Post Treatment Care Call List

AM APPOINTMENTS

Initials	*Patient*	*Appt. Time*	*TXT Completed*	*Phone Numbers*	

PM APPOINTMENTS

Initials	*Patients*	*Appt. Time*	*TXT Completed*	*Phone Numbers*	

Sample Smile Questionnaire

May we help you have YOUR best smile?

Please take a few minutes to answer the following questions so that we can help you have the smile you have always wanted!

Patient Name: ______________________________

Date: ______________________________

Are you able to chew and speak well?

☐ Yes ☐ No

Do you like the shape of your teeth?

☐ Yes ☐ No

Are your teeth ...

Chipped?	☐ Yes | ☐ No
Protruding?	☐ Yes | ☐ No
Crowded?	☐ Yes | ☐ No
Worn?	☐ Yes | ☐ No
Spaced Apart?	☐ Yes | ☐ No

What do you like the best about your smile?

____

____

Do you like the color of your teeth?

☐ Yes ☐ No

What do you like least about your smile?

Would you like to change the appearance of your teeth by:

a. Reshaping them? ☐ Yes ☐ No
b. Straightening them? ☐ Yes ☐ No
c. Whitening them? ☐ Yes ☐ No

Did your last dentist ever review long term goals for your dental health?

☐ Yes | ☐ No

Share with us why you left your last dentist?

Have you ever experienced a dental emergency?

☐ Yes | ☐ No

Please share any additional comments or suggestions.

Excellence in Service

Amazing customer service is what (Dental Office) is all about!

Satisfied Customers	Dissatisfied Customers
Customers will spend up to 10% more for a product when they receive optimal service	When customer service is poor, 91% of customers will not return
When a customer received optimal service, on average, they will tell 9-12 people about it	When a customer received poor service, on average, they will tell up to 20 people about it
When upsets and complaints are handled immediately, customers will purchase from that company again	After receiving poor service, 9% of customers will leave without complaining and simply not come back

5 Primary Reasons For Customer Complaints

1. Customer did not receive what he/she perceived as promised
2. Employee was rude, short or disrespectful
3. Employee exhibited a negative attitude
4. Employees did not ask what their needs were, and if asked, did not listen
5. Customer perceives employees did not go out of their way to service them

How Do We Consistently Provide Optimal Patient Service

Confirm: Confirm All appointments with a smile, optimize every appointment for accuracy, have new patients arrive 15 minutes early to complete and input paperwork, call patient on their cell phone if they are 5 minutes late

Phones: Answer every call by the 2nd ring and smile before answering. Be clear and speak slowly so patient hears your name, say "Thank you for calling (Dental Office), this is Megan, I can help you", end the verbiage with the tone of your voice going up to sound welcoming. Be warm and courteous and be prepared to get all new patient information the first time. Quotes are never given over the phone. Schedule patient to come in for a complimentary consultation with the Doctor. ALL information received goes in appointment note.

First Impressions: Always make eye contact and smile to every patient as soon as they walk through the door, even if you are on a call or with another patient. Introduce yourself to the new patient or existing patient if you do not know them. Constantly check your schedule for the next patient who will be coming in, review their picture so you can welcome them by name. All team members shake the patient's hand when you introduce yourself and welcome them to the practice or let them know it is great to see them again. Offer All patients water, snacks and bathroom.

New Patient Tour: Show enthusiasm and create excitement when walking a new patient through the practice. Introduce the new patient to each team member and address the team member as an expert in what they do. Excitedly show off any technology utilized in the practice.

Amenities Menu: Hand Every patient an amenities menu and ask if there is anything they would like from the list. Make a note in the patient file so you have it waiting for them, on the chair, at their next visit.

Asking Questions and Listening: Always find out what is *emotionally* important to the patient. What do they value, believe, fear, past dental experiences, events, vacations, outings, family get-togethers, do they have coming up in the next few months. What concerns, pain points, and interests do they have about their smile and health? What medications are they on that could be linked to their periodontal problems? What has a medical Doctor diagnosed them with? When did they last fill out a smile questionnaire? What is important to them? Did you provide a shade guide and mirror and ask the patient to tell you their teeth shade? These are emotional concerns for the patient and 90% of the time; people make decisions emotionally then justify it with logic. Ask questions and create scenarios using all of their senses. Input ALL the information in the patient file to discuss at future visits.

Hand Off: A patient should ALWAYS be accompanied by a team member through the office. At no time, should a patient ever walk through the practice alone. Every team member will hand off the patient to the next team member especially in hygiene. The Doctor is to always wait for the hand off from the hygienist. All team members follow the hand off guidelines and checklist of items to discuss in the hand off. All hand offs are done in the operatory, facing the patient vs. in the hallway or Doctor's office. People listen 100% of the time when they are being talked about.

Asking For Referrals: Have a referral card attached to every patient route slip. Throughout the appointment, compliment the patient on what a Great Job they are doing. Keep attaching positive feelings to the patient and their experience with the team and practice. At the end of the appointment, ask the patient how their experience was on a scale of 1-10. Whatever their response, always ask, what we could have done differently to make their experience better for them. Thank them for their input and let them know we love patients like them, ask them if they have any family and friends they would like to refer and hand them a care to share card. Explain the benefits to both themselves and the new patient Hand the patient off to the treatment coordinator. Input the feedback in patient notes for future visit.

The Object of the Patient Interview:

~ To establish immediate rapport
~ To establish trust and likeability
~ To understand our patient's model of the world and what they value
~ To discover how our patient processes information through their senses
~ To determine our patient's buying strategies

How do we discover what is important to our patients? Smile Questionnaire.

1. ____.

2. . ____.

3. . ____.

4. . ____.

5. . ____.

Clarification of Responses Using Key Words: Creating An Emotional Connection

~ What I hear you saying is............Tell me more about that...

~ What else?

~ What will that do for you?

~ How long have you been dealing with this pain/discomfort?

~ What have you not been able to do because of this?

~ What will you finally be able to do once we have fixed this? What will that do for you?

~ So, is it fair to say, that it's important for you to have this fixed?

~ What stops you from.....

~ What would happen if........(Creating Possibility)

Systems

Managing Systems, NOT People

When was the last time you experienced frustration at the office? What event led to that frustration? Is it frustrating when others do not follow through with what they say they are going to do?

We can chalk these disappointments up to two things: Missing Agreements or Broken Agreements. The good news is that we can manage both.

Managing by Systems = Managing via Agreements:

Many of our frustrations, disappointments, as well as chaos between team members, originates from miscommunication and/or misunderstandings.

Success in our business is built on trust. Trust comes from the decisions and agreements we make with ourselves and with each other. When we choose to follow through with our decisions and agreements, we establish integrity for our teams and ourselves.

Upholding our agreements ensures accountability, desired outcomes and measurable results. In turn, these outcomes lead to a gratifying work environment AND employee/employer security.

Managing with agreements vs. managing people, centers on the effective performance of the team. It eliminates unnecessary emotional upsets in the workplace.

How it works

Most agreements in our practices are expected or unnoticed—UNTIL they are broken and frustration arises.

Agreement always include:

1. WHAT the expectation or desired result is
2. WHO the commitment involves or could involve
3. WHERE the agreement is to be executed
4. HOW the commitment should be carried out, if there are pertinent specifications
5. WHEN is the commitment completion date (By-When)

Agreements Tracker

This final component is really the key to the success of this system. The tracker should be customized to suit the needs of the team. It can be as simple as a designated notebook or a tracking document on the computer. Tracking these commitments keeps the entire team in INTEGRITY, on track, moving forward, resulting in peace, harmony and more effective use of the team's time and energy, creating a 5-Star Experience for your patients.

The agreement tracker is managed by one team member to maintain accountability, continuity and accountability.

The difference between managing with systems vs managing people is that the focus is placed on the condition of your commitments and performance and not personality or personal preferences. This system allows work to be work, removing the more personal, sometimes distracting emotional upsets from the work environment.

Success Calendar—Front Office

Success Calendar

Monday	Tuesday	Wednesday	Thursday	Friday
3 8-10am Confirmation Calls 10-12 Insurance Verification Calls Call Unscheduled Txt Plans (1 week) Send Recare Reminder (4 Weeks)	4 8-10am Confirmation Calls 10-12 Insurance Verification Calls Call Unscheduled Txt Plan (1week)	8-10am Confirmation Calls 10-12 Insurance Verification Calls Call Unscheduled Txt Plans (1 week) Call Past Due Recare Reminder Call Recare (2 weeks)	8-10am Confirmation Calls 10-12 Insurance Verification Calls Call Unscheduled Txt Plans (1 week) Send Referral Thank You Cards	Expired Benefits Letter Sent Expired In House Savings Letter Sent
8-10am Confirmation Calls 10-12 Insurance Verification Calls Call Unscheduled Txt Plans (1 week) Send Recare Reminder (4 Weeks)	8-10am Confirmation Calls 10-12 Insurance Verification Calls Call Unscheduled Txt Plans (1 week)	8-10am Confirmation Calls 10-12 Insurance Verification Calls Call Unscheduled Txt Plans (1 week) Call Past Due Recare Reminder Call Recare (2 Weeks)	8-10am Confirmation Calls 10-12 Insurance Verification Call Call Unscheduled Txt Plans (1 week) Send Referral Thank You Cards	
8-10am Confirmation Calls 10-12 Insurance Verificaiton Calls Call Unscheduled Txt Plans (1 week) Send Recare Reminder (4 Weeks)	8-10am Confirmation Calls 10-12 Insurance Verification Calls Call Unscheduled Txt Plans (1 week)	8-10am Confirmation Calls 10-12 Insurance Verification Calls Call Unscheduled Txt Plans (1 week) Call Past Due Recare Reminder Call Recare (2 Weeks)	8-10am Confirmation Calls 10-12 Insurance Verification Calls Call Unscheduled Txt Plans (1 week) Send Referral Thank You Cards	
8-10am Confirmation Calls 10-12 Insurance Verification Calls Call Unscheduled Txt Plans (1 week) Send Recare Reminder (4 Weeks)	8-10am Confirmation Calls 10-12 Insurance Verification Calls Call Unscheduled Txt Plans (1 week)	8-10am Confirmation Calls 10-12 Insurance Verification Calls Call Unscheduled Txt Plans (1 week) Call Past Due Recare Reminder Call Recare (2 Weeks)	8-10am Confirmation Calls 10-12 Insurance Verification Calls Call Unscheduled Txt Plans (1 week) Send Referral Thank You Cards	
8-10am Confirmation Calls 10-12 Insurance Verification Calls Call Unscheduled Txt Plans (1 week) Send Recare Reminder (4 Weeks)	8-10am Confirmation Calls 10-12 Insurance Verification Calls Call Unscheduled Txt Plans (1 week)	8-10am Confirmation Calls 10-12 Insurance Verification Calls Call Unscheduled Txt Plans (1 week) Call Past Due Recare Reminder Call Recare (2 Weeks) Send Birthday Cards	8-10am Confirmation Calls 10-12 Insurance Verification Calls Call Unscheduled Txt Plans (1 week) Send Referral Thank You Cards	

Success Calendar—Office Manager

Success Calendar

Monday	Tuesday	Wednesday	Thursday	Friday
Practice Analysis, New Patient, Payment Agreements, Power Pay agreements, Monitor Hygiene Statistics Collection Calls	New Patient List Referral Report Hygiene & Unscheduled Txt Calls Collection Calls	Limited Exam Patients w/o prophy	Referred out patients w/o return visit appointment	
Hygiene & Unscheduled Txt Calls Cancellation & No Show List Unscheduled Appointment List Monitor Hygiene Statistics Collection Calls	Collection Calls			
Hygiene & Unscheduled Txt Calls Cancellation & No Show List Monitor Hygiene Statistics Collection Calls	Collection Calls		Referred out patients w/o return visit appointment	
Hygiene & Unscheduled Txt Calls Cancellation & No Show List Monitor Hygiene Statistics	Collection Calls	Limited exam patients w/o prophy		
Hygiene & Unscheduled Txt Calls Cancellation & No Show List Collection Calls	Collection Calls			

INSURANCE VERIFICATION FORM

Payor ID# ________________Date Called: _________________ Appointment Date:_________________
Insurance Name: ________________________________ Insurance Phone #: ________________________
Claim Address: _________________________________ Rep Name: ______________________________
_________________________________ Completed By: __________________________

Subscriber Name: ________________________________ Employer/Group Name: ____________________
Subscriber SS# __________________ DOB__________ ID #________________ Group # __________________
Patient Name: ______________________ DOB: ________________
Effective Date: ______________ Calendar Yr ( ) Other ( ): __________________________
Yearly Maximum: ________________________ Amount Used: ________________
Deductible: Single _______ Family ______ Ded Met: _______ Single Coverage/Family Coverage
Deductible applies to All: ________ Deductible applies to Basic & Major: _________

Coordination of Benefits: Standard/B-Day Rule ( ) or Non-Duplication ( )
In-Network/Contracted Fees: ______ Out-of-Network/Standard Fees: ______ Fee Schedule: _________

Preventive _________% Basic _________% Endo ( ) Perio ( ) O.S ( ) Major __________%

PLEASE BE AS SPECIFIC AS POSSIBLE

Prophy (1110/1120) _________________ Pall ER TX (9110) ______%____________TX same day:Yes/No XRays only
Exam (0120/0150) __________________ Lim EX (0140) _______%_____________ TX same day:Yes/No XRays only BWX(0274)
_______________________ Eligible? __________ pt HX ___________
FMX/Pano(0210/0330) _______________ Eligible? __________ pt HX ___________
Fluoride(1203/1204) ________________ Age Limit: _________ Eligible? _________
Sealants(1351) ______% ______________ Bicuspid( )Molars( ) Age Limit:_____ Eligible?_____
Perio Maint(4910) _______% Freq:_____________ Replace Prophy? ______ Notes: ________________________________
FMD(4355) ________% Freq:____________ Replace Prophy?_______ Eligible? ______ Notes: ___________________
SRP(4341) ________% Freq: ______________(4 Quads Same Day)?_______ Eligible? ______ Notes: ________________
Arestin(4381) _________% Freq:______________ Notes: _______________________________________
Gingivectomy(4210) _______% Freq:____________ Notes:_______________________________________

Missing Tooth Clause (MTC)? _________ Waiting Periods? ________ Prior Auth Sugg Over?__________

Posterior Composites(2391) ________% (or) Downgraded to Amalgam ( ) Freq: ________________
Porcelain Crowns Downgraded? (2740)_______ (2750)________ (6750)_________ Notes: _______________________
Replacement Policy: Denture________ Crown_______ Bridge________ Partials _________
Pays on: PREP/SEAT
Crown BuildUp(2950)________% Crown same day?__________ Notes:_________________________________
Pulp Vitality Test(0460)______%________________ Pulp Cap(3110/3120)_____%____________________________

Implants(6010)____% Feq:________ Notes:______________ Implant CRN(6058/6059)_____%Freq:___________
Vizilite(0431)______% Freq:________ Notes:_________ Nitrous(9230)____% Freq:_________
Occl Guard(9940)_____% Freq:_________ Notes: __________________ Occl Adj(9952)______% req:__________
IV Sedation(9241)_______% Freq:_______________
Non-IV Sedation:Oral Sedation(9248) _______% Freq:____________ Notes:________________________
ORTHO:_______% Deductible_______ Age Limit:__________________ Maximum $_________________
Pays Out:____

Filling 2 Surface Checklist

Filling 2 Surface Checklist **Patient Name:** ______________________

Procedures	Time (Mins)
Greeting patient in reception area with handshake	
Seating Patient	
Handoff to Patient (to review today's procedure)	
Update & review medical history	
Inquire about any dental concerns (any questions patient may have)	
Take blood pressure	
Consent form	
Open instruments (set up)	
Call Dr. on radio	
Handoff to Doctor	
Apply topical/doctor numbs	
Offer amenities	
Waiting for patient to be numb	
Call doctor on radio	
Drill/prepare teeth	
Restore	
Post-op instructions reviewed	
Towel to patient	
Confirm today's treatment in the computer and set appt complete	
Finish notes in Dentrix	
Schedule next appt.	
***Hand-Off** to tx coordinator or check out	
Give patient router and hhx form to tx coordinator	
Decontaminate treatment rooms	
Sterilize instruments	
Set up treatment rooms for next patient	

Extra
Extra
Extra
Extra

Cerec Visit Checklist

Cerec Visit Checklist **Patient Name:** ______________________

Procedures	Time (Mins)
Greeting patient in reception area with handshake	
Seating patient	
Handoff to Patient (to review today's procedure)	
Update & review medical history	
Inquire about any dental concerns (any questions patient may have)	
Take blood pressure	
Consent form	
Call Dr. on radio	
Handoff to Doctor	
Apply topical / doctor numbs	
Scan with doctor or self on cerec computer	
Waiting for patient to get numb	
Doctor or self cleans image on cerce computer	
Call Dr. on radio	
Drill/prepare teeth	
Restore	
Pack cord	
Final scan of restored tooth	
Doctor designs crown	
Milling process	
Adjustments to crown	
Xray and patient approval	
Preparing crown to go in oven	
Baking time	
Air dry time	
Try in with patient	
Call Dr. on radio	
Final check for cementation	
Prepare for cementation, cement crown, clean excess cement	
Xray for final	
Post-op instructions reviewed	
Towel to patient	
Confirm today's treatment in the computer and set appt complete	
Finish notes in Dentrix	
Make next appointment (if needed)	
***Hand-Off** to tx coordinator or check out	
Give patient router and hhx form to tx coordinator	
Decontaminate treatment rooms	
Sterilize instruments	
Set up treatment rooms for next patient	

Extra
Extra
Extra
Extra

Crown Delivery Visit Checklist

Crown Delivery Visit Checklist **Patient Name:** ____________________

Procedures	Time (Mins)
Greeting patient in reception area with handshake	
Seating Patient	
Handoff to Patient (to review today's procedure)	
Inquire about any dental concerns (any questions patient may have)	
Offer amenities (water, pillow, blanket, etc.)	
Remove provisional crown(s)	
Try in permanent crown(s) and make any adjustments needed	
Take pre-cementation x-ray patient approval for cement	
Call Dr. on radio	
Handoff to Doctor	
Doctor checks overall fit of crown	
Prepared crown of cementation/cement crown/clean excess cement	
Take post-cementation x-ray	
Post-op instructions reviewed	
Towel to patient	
Confirm today's treatment in the computer and set appt complete	
Finish notes in Dentrix	
Schedule next appt.	
***Hand-Off** to tx coordinator or check out	
Give patient router and hhx form to tx coordinator	
Decontaminate treatment rooms	
Sterilize instruments	
Set up treatment rooms for next patient	

Extra
Extra
Extra
Extra

Delivery of Night Guard Checklist

Delivery of Night Guard Checklist **Patient Name:** ______________________

Procedures	Time (Mins)
Greeting patient in reception area with handshake	
Seating patient	
Offer Amenities	
Handoff to Patient (to review today's procedure)	
Call Dr. if needed	
Try night guard, place in warm water if needed. (Assistant/Dr)	
Adj (if needed)	
Pt approves	
Towel to patient	
Finish notes in Dentrix	
Confirm today's treatment in the computer and set apt complete	
Schedule if needed or further Tx	
***Hand-Off** to tx coordinator or check out	
Give patient router and hhx form to tx coordinator	
Decontaminate treatment rooms	
Sterilize instruments	
Set up treatment rooms for next patient	

Extra

Extra

Extra

Extra

Lab Crown Checklist

Lab Crown Checklist **Patient Name:** ______________________

Procedures	Time (Mins)
Greeting patient in reception area with handshake	
Seating Patient	
Offer Amenities	
Handoff to Patient (to review today's procedure)	
Update & review medical history	
Inquire about any dental concerns (any questions patient may have)	
Take blood pressure	
Consent form	
Open instruments (set up)	
Call Dr. on radio	
Handoff to Doctor (With EM)	
Apply topical / Doctor numbs	
Waiting for patient to be numb (Take pre-impression). Offer water.	
Drill w/ existing crown decay yes or no	
Drill w/ no crown decay yes or no	
Cord	
Restore (without existing crn) build up yes or no	
Final impression (4-5 min) Finish notes	
Bite registration	
Make temp. (start to finish). Shade pick	
Post-op instructions reviewed	
Towel to patient	
Confirm today's treatment in the computer and set appt complete	
Schedule next appt.	
Finish notes in Dentrix	
***Hand-Off** to tx coordinator or check out	
Give patient router and hhx form to tx coordinator	
Decontaminate treatment rooms	
Sterilize instruments	
Set up treatment rooms for next patient	

Extra
Extra
Extra
Extra

Limited Exam Checklist

Limited Exam Checklist **Patient Name:** ____________________

Procedures	**Time (Mins)**
Greeting patient in reception area with handshake	
Seating patient	
Handoff to Patient (to review today's procedure) questions	
Update &review medical history	
Inquire about any dental concerns (any questions patient may have)	
Take blood pressure	
Take x-rays/photos	
Open instruments (set up)	
Call doctor on radio	
Handoff to Doctor	
Exam/x-ray/phot review	
Towel to patient	
Confirm today's treatment in the computer and set appt complete	
Finish notes in Dentrix	
Make the next appointment (if needed)	
***Hand-Off** to tx coordinator or check out	
Give patient router and hhx form to tx coordinator	
Decontaminate treatment rooms	
Sterilize instruments	
Set up treatment rooms for next patient	

Extra

Extra

Extra

Extra

Preliminary Examination for Dentures Checklist

Premliminary Impressions for Dentures Checklist **Patient Name:** ______________

Procedures	**Time (Mins)**
Greeting patient in reception area with handshake	
Seating patient	
Offer Amenities	
Handoff to Patient (to review today's procedure) questions	
Pick tray size	
Upper/Lower alginate impression	
Towel to patient	
Finish notes in Dentrix	
Confirm today's treatment in the computer and set apt complete	
Schedule Custom trays.	
***Hand-Off** to tx coordinator or check out	
Give patient router and hhx form to tx coordinator	
Pour models in lab (lab slip)	
Decontaminate treatment rooms	
Sterilize instruments	
Set up treatment rooms for next patient	

Extra

Extra

Extra

Extra

Root Canal Checklist

RCT Checklist **Patient Name:** ____________________

Procedures	**Time (Mins)**
Greeting patient in reception area with handshake	
Seating Patient	
Handoff to Patient (to review today's procedure)	
Update & review medical history	
Inquire about any dental concerns (any questions patient may have)	
Take blood pressure	
Consent form	
Open instruments (set up)	
Call Dr. on radio	
Handoff to Doctor	
Apply topical / Doctor numbs	
Offer amenities (water, blanket, pillow, etc.)	
Waiting for patient to get numb	
Call Dr. on radio	
Drill/prepare teeth	
Restore/RCT	
Post-op instructions reviewed	
Towel to patient	
Confirm today's treatment in the computer and set appt complete	
Finish notes in Dentrix	
Make the next appointment (if needed)	
***Hand-Off** to tx coordinator or check out	
Give patient router and hhx form to tx coordinator	
Decontaminate treatment rooms	
Sterilize instruments	
Set up treatment rooms for next patient	

Extra

Extra

Extra

Extra

Teeth Try-in for Dentures/Partials Checklist

Teeth try-in For Dentures/Partials Checklist **Patient Name:** ____________________

Procedures	Time (Mins)
Greeting patient in reception area with handshake	
Seating	
Offer Amenities	
Handoff to Patient (to review today's procedure)	
Call Dr. for Teeth try-in	
Dr. focuses/places denture/partial	
Pt approves	
Towel to patient	
Finish notes in Dentrix	
Confirm today's treatment in the computer and set apt complete	
Schedule Denture Delivery	
***Hand-Off** to tx coordinator or check out	
Give patient router and hhx form to tx coordinator	
Write lab slip	
Decontaminate treatment rooms	
Sterilize instruments	
Set up treatment rooms for next patient	

Extra

Extra

Extra

Extra

Correspondence

List of Correspondence Letters

~ Collection: 60, 75, 90, Final collection
~ Associate joining practice
~ Dismissal
~ End of year insurance utilization
~ Excused absence
~ Failed appointment no fee
~ Failed appointment charging fee
~ In-House Savings Program expiring
~ Insurance payment sent to patient
~ New Year insurance utilization
~ Overdue recall
~ Reactivation
~ Thank you to patient for referral
~ Thank you to Doctor for referral
~ Uncompleted treatment
~ Welcome

How to Respond to Online Reviews

Quickly acknowledge, celebrate, and express gratitude for the positive reviews, and acknowledge, respond to, and learn from any negative reviews. Responding appropriately, quickly, and authentically to online reviews illustrates to potential patients that you care enough about your practice and your relationships to engage with the people you serve.

Don't be afraid of the occasional negative review. Believe it or not, an occasional negative review can actually contribute to your online credibility. It demonstrates that the review process hasn't been "gamed" or faked, and potential patients are more likely to trust the reviews they read about your practice. A negative review will stand in bold contrast to your positive reviews, adding authenticity to your profile.

Here are the best strategies for responding to online reviews.

- **Never respond when you're angry or defensive.**
- **Respond as quickly as you can**, to illustrate your commitment to an ongoing relationship.
- **Always respond politely and positively**—even to the worst reviews.
- **Thank the patient** for their review, and express that you value their feedback
- **Keep responses brief and professional**. Readers don't care about details, they care that you take notice.
- **Don't offer any free service** or other inducements to reward positive reviews.
- **Don't defend yourself from minor criticism**. It makes you look petty. If it occurs, own it, apologize if necessary, and let it go.
- **Do not argue or try to change the reviewer's mind**. Just be positive, thankful, and sincere. Do not set the stage for a "flame" war – express your commitment to customer satisfaction.
- **Don't discuss anything specific or personal** pertaining to the patient or treatment you provided them — this puts you in violation of HIPAA rules

Example response to a positive review:
Thank you for taking the time to give us such a great review! (Dental Office) values your feedback and uses it to continue to improve the services we offer. Have an amazing day!

Example response to a negative review:
Thank you for your feedback. We sincerely apologize that we did not meet your expectations during your last visit/call/email/etc. That's not the level of service we intend to provide our valued patients. We take all reviews seriously, and will use your feedback to improve our customer service. Thanks again, and have an amazing day.

Team: Morning Huddle, Team Meeting

Morning Huddle Mastermind

Date of Daily Mastermind: ______________ **Conversation Topics:**_______________

Previous Days #'s	Office Production			
	Goal		Actual	
Doctors				
Hygiene				
Treatment Presented:	$		Treatment Accepted:	$

1. What worked well yesterday?

2. What was missing?

3. Where were gaps in the schedule? Why?

Projections for Today______________ **Conversation Today:**__________________

Previous Days #'s	Office Production	
	Goal	Scheduled
Doctors		
Hygiene		

# of Open Time Slots:
Who is filling the spaces and HOW?

- Note patients with special needs.. (pre-med, latex allergy's etc)
- Unscheduled tx plans? Perio required? Update dates, providers notes, notice changes that work in the practices favor..
- Patients that have $$ Due?
- Referrals? Who should be asked and remember to ASK
- Yesterday's referrals and what worked?
- Notable patient events? (birthdays, anniversary's, grads, losses)
- Time slots can emergency patients be placed and with whom?
- Patients without hygiene appts? Family members of patients?

Prepare for Tomorrow______________ **Team Discussion:**___________________

	Office Production	
	Goal	Scheduled
Doctors		
Hygiene		

Number of openings:___________
How/Who can fill:____________
Concerns with tomorrows schedule
Are patients charts complete?
Patients with an open balance?

Morning Huddles

The most important part of your day is the ten to fifteen minutes spent each morning before your patients are seen. This valuable time reduces numerous problems that can arise throughout the day. This is not a time to discuss staff issues. This is the time to discuss today's patients. Keep your answering machine on during your meeting. This time needs to be uninterrupted!

ITEMS NEEDED FOR MEETING

- Copy of today's schedule for all Team Members
- Emergency Patient Forms/New Patients Forms
- Production report for Doctor/Hygiene
- Patient communications: Birthdays, Anniversaries, Vacations, etc....
- Balance & Financial challenges for patients

When reviewing the overall schedule, here are some important questions to ask:

1. Are we at our goal today?
2. If not, where do we have opportunity to add same-day service or work in other patients?
3. Do any of our hygiene patients need treatment? Do any of our restorative patients need a hygiene visit?
4. Who are our new patients? How did they hear about our office?
5. Have any of today's patients referred other patients recently? Make sure to thank them.
6. What patients are not confirmed?
7. Is everything delivered and ready to go for lab cases tomorrow?
8. Where is the best place to fit in emergency patients?

Appointment or Scheduling Coordinator

- Discuss yesterday's schedule (Do not focus on the negative)
- Review Doctor's Production Schedule (Unscheduled time units)
- Review Hygiene Production Schedule (Unscheduled time units)
- New patient information (include new emergency patients). This breakdown should include possible motivators and concerns, reason for the appointment, any special needs or concerns, and how the patient was referred
- Highlight all patients due for a health history update
- Highlight all patients who need a Smile Questionaire
- Patients who should receive a thank you for their referral
- Patients who waited more than 10 minutes at a previous visit
- Patients who chronically show up late
- Highlight patients birthdays within 60 days, anniversaries, any relevant events

Financial Coordinator

- Discuss any patients who can express pay today
- Discuss any patients who have balances owing today (routing slips & treatment plans)
- Discuss any patients who have past due balances and are getting additional work today (getting payment before seated with the Doctor)
- Review patients with credits to use towards treatment diagnosed today

Hygienist

- Review charts in advance
- Review hygiene production goal vs. production scheduled for the day
- Identify patients' emotional motivators, concerns, connection points
- Highlight patients who are due for FMX, Pano & BWX
- Highlight any family past due for a hygiene visit
- Highlight patients who need pre-medication
- Highlight patients who need updated health history
- Highlight patients due for periodontal probing
- Highlight patients who have outstanding restorative treatment plans
- Identify patients who can benefit from fluoride, desensitizer, sealants
- Optimize next day appointments

Assistants

- Identify patients' emotional motivators, concerns, connection points
- Verify scheduled treatment matches treatment plans—make necessary corrections
- Identify openings for emergency appointments
- Verify all lab cases are checked in for the next two days appointments
- Highlight patients needing pre-medication
- Using patient notes, highlight or add patients requesting nitrous oxide, blanket, pillow, music genre, etc.
- Highlight patients to schedule for next hygiene visit. Can they be added into today's schedule?
- Other services that can be offered— teeth whitening, Invisalign, night guards, cosmetic procedures

Office Manager

- Discuss if yesterday's production & collection goals were reached – review revised goals if not met
- Discuss today's production scheduled vs. production goal for each provider
- Discuss opportunities
- Have anyone share a positive thought for the day
- Close meeting on time

Benefits of consistent morning huddles

- Improved organization by planning the day instead of just letting it happen
- Understanding & discussing each patient's needs in advance
- Confirming that all necessary supplies and lab cases are ready
- Increased profitability by having the entire team aware of patients who have not scheduled and utilizing the information to motivate patients to accept treatment
- Office Manager keeping all team members informed of daily production goals vs. scheduled production and reinforcing team effort to achieve these goals

Team Meeting Agenda

Date: __________ 2017

Team Meeting Leader: ______________________________

Recorder: ______________________________

Current Month: ______________________________

	Current	Goal
Gross Production	$	$
Scheduled Production	$	$
Adjustments	$	$
Net Production	$	$
Collections	$	$
Collections %		98% adj prod
Over The Counter Collections %		40-45% of adj prod
New Patients	Unsourced	
Production Avg Per New Patient	$	
Doctor Treatment Accepted	$	$
Doctor Treatment Unaccepted	$	$
Doctor Treatment Accepted %		70-80%
Doctor Production Total	$	$
Doctor Production Per Hour	$	$
Doctor Broken Appts or Open Time		<5%

Hygiene Treatment Accepted	$	$
Hygiene Treatment Unaccepted	$	$
Hygiene Treatment Accepted %		70-80%
Hygiene Production Total		
Hygiene Production Per Hour	$	$
Hygiene % of Gross Production		30%
Hygiene Broken Appts or Open Time		<8%
Recall Rate %		95%
Retention Rate		90%
Perio Rate %		50%
Fluoride Rate %		

Next Month:

Scheduled Production	$	$

Next Meeting: ______________________________

Meeting Leader: ______________________________

Recorder: ______________________________

Team Recognition Bravo Awards

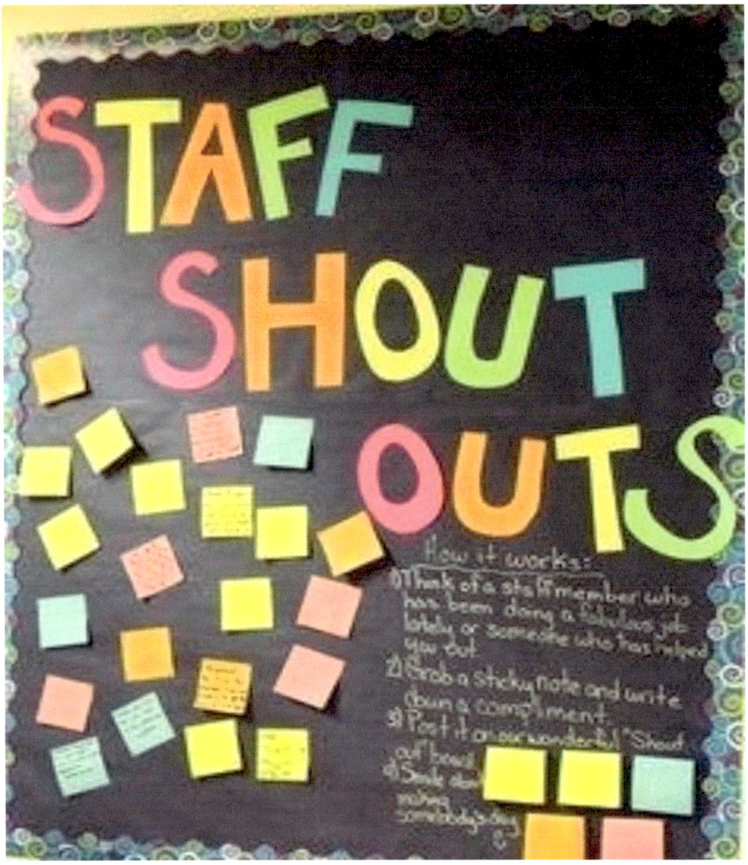

At each team meeting, recognize your team members who make an extra effort to solve problems in creative and innovative ways. Acknowledge those who take the time to help another team member out. Empower your team by recognizing them for going above and beyond the expected.

Monthly Team Member Recognition

Attitude

Sense Of Humor

"Can Do" Attitude

Source Of Positivity To Others

Passionate Enthusiasm

Open-Minded

Leadership

Solution-Minded

Takes Responsibility For Communication

Confident

Risk Taker

Recognizes Others

Communication

Overcomes Objections

Acknowledges Others Point Of Views

Creates & Builds Value

Speaks Less & Listens More

Seeks Confirmation Of Understanding

High Five Awards

Action-Oriented

Detail -Oriented

Get The Job Done

Do More Than The Expected Job

Great Team Player

How to Give a Feedback Sandwich

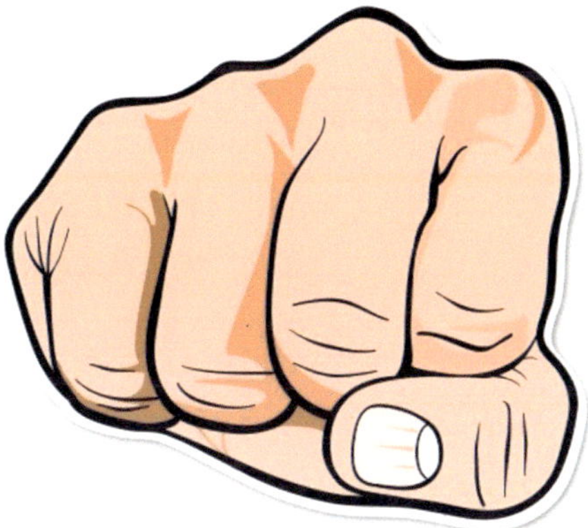

How to Give a Feedback Sandwich

Tell them one of two things that were right.

Give them a stretch. What can they improve? Use sensory based words.

Tell them, overall, how good it was.

To be effective make sure feedback follows these simple rules:

Be in the same physical locations and state as the exercise.

Give the feedback quickly, within five minutes.

Receiver: No justifications. Just say, "Thank you."

Goals

Knowing Your KPI's

- Total active patients
- Active patient value
- Number of new patients
- New patient conversion rate
- New patient value
- Net patient growth
- Total office collections
- Collection ratio
- Collections at time of scheduling/service
- Total office production
- Fee for service vs. Insurance production
- Average production per patient
- Accounts receivable balance
- Months on the book
- Average production per hour for each doctor
- Restorative case acceptance
- Average production per hour for each doctor
- Restorative case acceptance
- Hygiene production to practice production
- Perio production to hygiene production
- Average production per hour for each hygienist
- Hygiene case acceptance
- Hygiene patients reappointed %
- Number of broken appointments for hygiene
- Number of broken appointments for doctor
- Overhead

Goals & Statistics for Your Practice

New/Active Patients

- ✓ 1,800 – 2,000 active patients per general dentist
- ✓ 90% patient retention through hygiene
- ✓ 10 – 20 new patients per dentist, per month
- ✓ 70% of new patients from internal marketing and referrals
- ✓ 8-10% yearly attrition rate

Production

- ✓ Average general dentist production: $300-500 per hour, depending on experience
- ✓ Average annual production per active patient: $500-700
- ✓ Average diagnosis per new patient: $2,500 minimum, with 50-65% acceptance rate
- ✓ Case acceptance: 60% - 80%
- ✓ 30-40% total office production from hygiene, with hygienists producing 3-4 times their compensation
- ✓ Up to 40% of production should come from new patients (average production per new patient report)
- ✓ Up to 10% of production from emergency patients
- ✓ Annual production per operatory: $250,000 per year
- ✓ Case acceptance: 60% - 80%

Collections	98% of Adjusted Production
✓ Over-the-Counter Collections	40-45% of Adjusted Production
✓ Accounts Receivable	1 Month on book
✓ Current	70% of Total Receivables
✓ 30 – 60 Days	<20% of Total Receivables
✓ 60 - 90 Days	<5% of Total Receivables
✓ 90+ Days	<5% of Total Receivables

Hygiene

- ✓ Hygiene should maintain > 90% re-care effectiveness each month
- ✓ 100% of patients should pre-appoint for their continuing care appointments
- ✓ Up to 50% of patients should be referred to a more intensive level of periodontal treatment
- ✓ 40-80% of doctor treatment coming out of the hygiene re-care chairs monthly
- ✓ Less than 10% loss through cancellations or broken appointments monthly

Marketing

- ✓ Implement three internal marketing plans and three external marketing plans, and work them simultaneously
- ✓ Encourage patients to review your practice online. 62% of patients use online reviews as a first step to find a new dentist, and 26% of insured patients are willing to visit a doctor outside their network if that doctor's reviews are higher than those of their in-network doctors
- ✓ Maximize website effectiveness as a marketing tool. Conversions can rise by 80% or more when video is used on a landing page
- ✓ Evaluate and improve telephone procedures, especially for calls placed "on hold." 60% of callers left on silent hold will hang up

Hitting Target Versus Goal

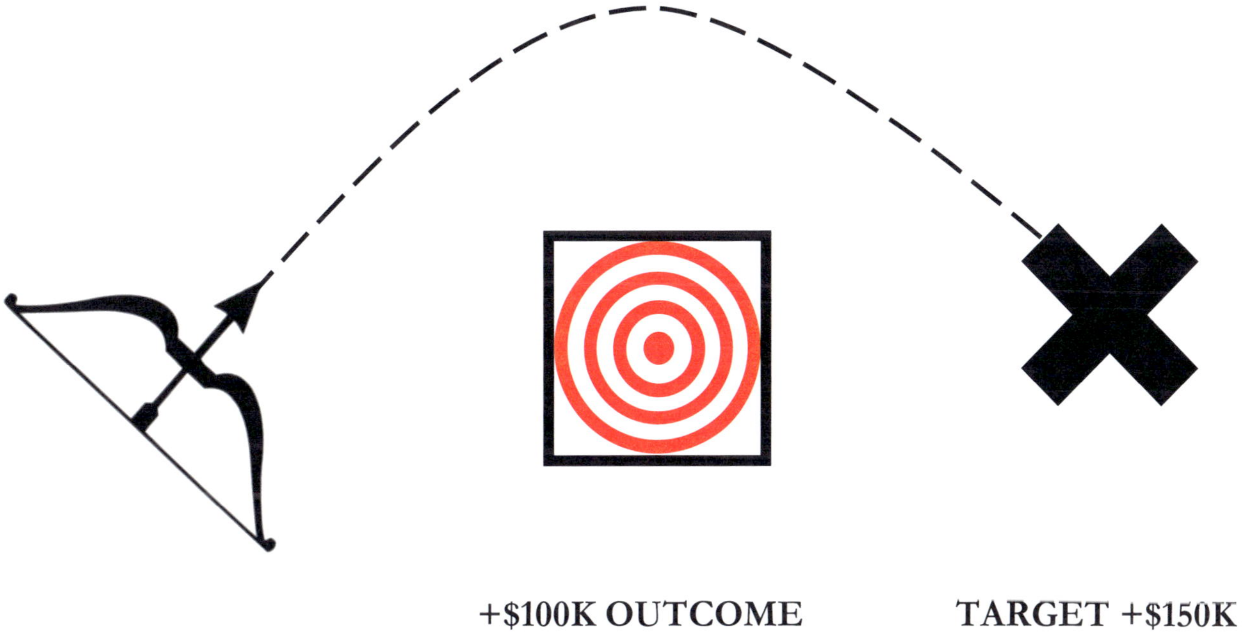

Production Goal Arrow

Our Goal For March

0

Day of Mo.	Date		
30		YOU HIT THE BONUS !!!	-
29			-
28			-
27			-
26			-
25			-
24			-
23			-
22			-
21			-
20			-
19			-
18			-
17			-
16			-
15			-
14			-
13			-
12			-
11			-
10			-
9			-
8			-
7			-
6			-
5			-
4			-
3			-
2			-
1			-

Color in the lines up to the line showing that amount. Write the day of the report you used next to the top line.

Collection Target Arrow

Our Goal For March

0

Day of Mo.	Date		
30		YOU HIT THE BONUS !!!	-
29			-
28			-
27			-
26			-
25			-
24			-
23			-
22			-
21			-
20			-
19			-
18			-
17			-
16			-
15			-
14			-
13			-
12			-
11			-
10			-
9			-
8			-
7			-
6			-
5			-
4			-
3			-
2			-
1			-

Color in the lines up to the line showing that amount. Write the day of the report you used next to the top line.

Inserting a Goal into the Future

1. Make sure the goal is SMART
2. Get the Last Step
3. Make an Internal Representation
4. Step into It – Associate
5. Adjust the Sub modalities
6. Step Out of It - Dissociate

Avatar Worksheet: Who Is My Ideal Patient?

Avatar Worksheet: Who Is My Ideal Patient?

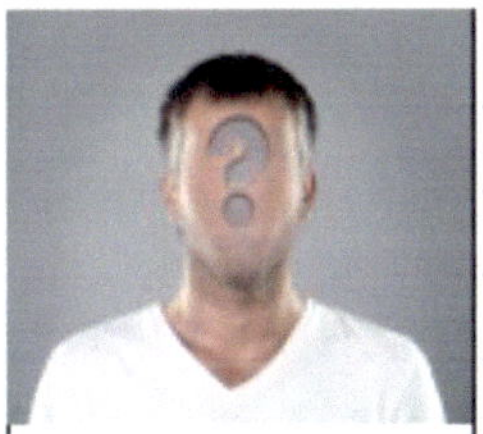

Photo

Name: ____________________

Gender: ____________ Age: ____________

Occupation: ____________________

Relationship Status: ____________________

Parents/Upbringing: ____________________

Location: ____________________

Identities: ____________________

Values: ____________________

Beliefs: ____________________

Capabilities: ____________________

Behaviors/Hobbies: ____________________

Possessions: ____________________

Struggles: ____________________

Pain Points: ____________________

Fears: ____________________

Desires: ____________________

Goals/Dreams: ____________________

Training Contacts

Keep in touch with us and with those at this training. Make note of all your contacts' information here.

Name	Phone	Email
Patrice Bonnell	602-980-3322	patrice@dmicoaching.com
Shelly Goff	480-273-7894	shelly@dmicoaching.com

Made in the USA
Las Vegas, NV
03 November 2026

57420365R00117